Love For God's Gra...

"God's Grace and Grit" lays out a Christ-centered path to create, and maybe more importantly, rebuild a solid marriage. Written from a biblical perspective, through the lens of experience of a marriage's messiness, and putting the reader directly in the process, Carolyn and Tiarra offer the tools, the exercises, the questions, and the challenges to help create the JOY in the marriage JOurneY.

~BRUCE PULVER – Author, Podcaster, TEDx speaker, and
Wordsmith https://abovethechatterourwordsmatter.com/

I believe THIS BOOK will transform marriages and relationships in ways we never thought possible! The clever writing style and storytelling makes it fun to remember what really matters in life and love. The tips are priceless. Thank you so much for writing a book that brings us back to a stronger foundation of beliefs and principles for a more balanced and fulfilled life!

~TINA CHANDLER – IFBB Professional Bodybuilder, Fitness
Coach, and Founder or NORMAL TO BE FIT® and
NORMAL TO BE FIT® Charitable Foundation.

Absolutely magnificent, such practical advice, and such beautiful perspectives. So uniquely written from the perspective of two strong women who have been through so much.

~SYLVIA MARUSYK – Author, Activational Mentor, and
International Keynote Speaker - http://mindbodyworks.ca/

I just want to sing you all's praises on emphasizing sometimes a marriage has to end for safety! Definitely an important aspect that can sometimes get lost in the idea that "God doesn't want divorce!" It's great to see encouragement to make a marriage work while acknowledging that sometimes it can't.

~LINDSEY BEEHEE – Author & Podcaster -
https://fearscapemedia.com/gabbpodcast/

This book speaks to men just as much as it does to women. As it focuses on marriage, you can use the ideologies within for any type of relationship. Amazing journey into the mind of how women think, and how precious they truly are.

~CURTIS BARNHILL – Up and Coming Author

Carolyn and Tiarra have done an amazing job of compiling a list of "Survival Tips" that is a MUST read for all women - single, engaged, married, or divorced. It is filled with fresh and practical advice that will encourage and challenge you.

~BETHANY CHAMBERS – Wife, Mother, and Passionate
Fitness Instructor

God's
GRACE & GRIT

God's
GRACE & GRIT

Surviving Your Fairytale

Carolyn Snelling
Tiarra Tompkins

Carpenter's Son Publishing

Published by Carpenter's Son Publishing, Franklin, Tennessee

Edited by Ann Tatlock

Developmental Edit By The Legacy Architect

Cover Design and Interior Design by Suzanne Lawing

Printed in the United States of America

978-1-954437-67-8

Dedicated to helping you survive your fairytale

*Be cheerful no matter what; pray all the time;
thank God no matter what happens. This is the way God
wants you who belong to Christ Jesus to live.*
~1 THESSALONIANS 5: 16-18 (MSG)

Contents

Read Me First

*O*nce upon a time, there were two sisters in Christ who wanted to in-spire others. They worked together to create a book that would give glory to God and provide people everywhere a biblical perspective on how to be more present in their marriages. They ran into just one problem. How would you, our beloved reader, tell our stories apart?!

We knew we needed something special, and it became a treasure hunt to find the best way to share these tips with you and prevent confusion. We landed on:

A ring for Carolyn

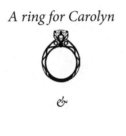

&

A crown for Tiarra

You will know we have switched when you see the ring or the crown.

We know that many of you may have survival tips of your own. Since we know that we can always learn, we would love to hear from you!

Please visit our website at www.GodsGraceAndGrit.com to share your survival tips, order books, and post prayers! This survival journey isn't just about some tips, it is about us each sharing what has led us to travel God's marriage road and the ways He equips us to survive and thrive in them!

We can't wait to read your stories and your survival tips. As always, may this book be a blessing, something that glorifies God alone, and something that helps you seek His face even more. Enjoy reading and remember you have our prayers and our love always.

Your Sisters in Christ,
Carolyn & Tiarra

Introduction

God's Grace Gives Grit

Be strong in the grace that is in Christ Jesus.
~2 TIMOTHY 2:1

*W*hen the Holy Spirit prompted me to update one of my previous books and republish it, I thought that would be my last book. My publisher connected me with a writer he believed would help me breathe new life into my young children's novel. With the connection made, it turned out that book was not meant to be updated. God put another sort of book on my heart, and it was a perfect time to enlist Tiarra Tompkins (The Legacy Architect) as my co-author. Her expertise in the book industry is without equal.

My heart's original intent for writing this inspirational guide was to provide encouragement to caregiving spouses. As soon as I described what was on my heart, Tiarra was on board with a resounding, "I love it!" I'm so grateful to God for her as this guide is stronger and more meaningful because of her contributions. She has a dynamic intellect and an energy for our Savior which manifests itself in powerful ways. I encourage you to read more of her story and servant's heart in her blog. You can find it in her bio at the back of the book with other resources we believe will help you on your journey.

As we talked more about what we believed the Holy Spirit was telling us to share, the audience expanded. We knew there was more to share and the people we were serving through this journey came to include married women, divorced women, single women, parents, as well as caregiving spouses. Much to our surprise, God expanded the audience even further to include men as well. Please take a minute to read the comments on the testimonial page. We were blown away by what these men had to say! That's our God!!

From there, I was on a quest for the perfect book cover. All authors want to create a book cover that will catch your eye and give you just a hint at what is inside. As I began my research, the delicate yet sturdy glass slipper caught my eye. Specifically, I marveled at the Glass Maker and what He used to make this infamous slipper endure the test of time. Glass is composed of sand, heated and melted to such a degree that it is beyond recognition of what it once was. It's amazing how the gritty nature of sand can make something so smooth and beautiful.

It's amazing how the gritty nature of sand can make something so smooth and beautiful.

Black sand reminds me of precious memories my husband, Bob, and I made on our trips to Hawaii, especially our wedding and honeymoon. Frolicking on the beach, body surfing in the crashing waves, snorkeling, and taking moonlight walks was an idyllic fairytale beginning.

After the honeymoon glow wanes, challenges of small and big proportions can arise. How do any of us survive these challenges? Our Glass Maker knew we would need His amazing grace and the strength He provides to face the things the enemy would use to attempt to keep us from our fairytales.

Tiarra and I invite you to join us on God's Survival Journey. We pray this guide, filled with our stories and the stories of others, will help you see the Glass Maker's grace in action. As for additional sustenance on the journey, we thought sharing the Fruit of the Spirit would be … well … fruitful. We thought it could be a fun treasure hunt for you to find the Fruit of the Spirit contained within some of the chapters. Here's a tree containing the "fruit."

Galatians 5:22-23

You might also find it helpful identifying which fruit you could "pick more often" to feed your marriage. We've also offered acrostics for each fruit that may help you remember their individual meaning.

Since this book is about surviving your fairytale, we have created fun and hopefully meaningful survival tips for each chapter.

The most valuable survival tool from God is His Word which the Holy Spirit has provided throughout. In considering survival and a reliance on God, we turn to none other than the apostle Paul. When Paul wrote 2 Timothy, he was in prison. This final letter could have adopted a depressing tone. He could have chosen a pity party for his last communique. Instead, he chose an attitude of encouragement and hope to share with his young protegee, Timothy, and the world.

For the Spirit God gave us does
not make us timid but gives us power,
love and self-discipline.
(2 Timothy 1:7)

You too can receive God's Grace and Grit; the choice is yours.

Cinderella's tale is one of my favorites but not because I was a charcoal-stained orphan with a dream for a new life. In fact, just the opposite. I was a spoiled brat. My parents indulged my every whim and presented countless opportunities for success. My response to their generosity was one of disrespect, disdain, and disgust. I treated them abominably. *God forgive me.* I was more like an evil stepsister. Had I known the love of Jesus as a kid, His words such as the following may have resonated. *"Children, obey your parents in the Lord, for this is right. 'Honor your father and mother'—which is the first commandment with a promise – 'so that it may go well with you and that you may enjoy long life on the earth'"* (Ephesians 6:1-3).

Thank God for allowing one of Pastor Rick Warren's best-selling books, *The Purpose Driven Life: What on Earth Am I Here For?*[1], to cross my dark path. The first four words in this life-changing book are, "It's not about you." [2] He offers these words in the context of life lived for God and others. Those four words are your first survival tip.

Survival Tip #1: It's Not About You

Time now to turn to my precious co-author. Tiarra, the forest floor is yours.

Survival Tip #1

It's Not About You

She comforts, encourages, and does him only good
and not evil all the days of her life.
~Proverbs 31:12 AMP

First, let me say that it is an honor to be able to share with you, our dear reader, the important things God has shared with us. I can't thank Carolyn enough for including me in this journey and I pray that it blesses you as it has blessed me.

Before we dive in, I want to ask you a question. Did you, or do you, have any expectations on what married life should be? Some of my first memories as a kid are watching beautiful princesses traverse danger into their happily ever after. What fairytales failed to show us is the hard work that is required of any relationship. Most animated versions of the Grimm's fairytales end in the "happily ever after," but we never see Cinderella doing the prince's laundry, nor do we see Snow White washing dishes and picking up dirty socks. If the fairytales we grew up on didn't give us the whole picture, then what does it mean to live happily ever after?

For me, it can be hard to swallow the words of our first survival tip. If we are being honest with ourselves, we know that there are many times when our actions speak louder than words and we miss a moment to give grace. We instead choose the path of MOST resistance and in that choice, we make a moment ALL ABOUT US. Has this happened to you? It is easier than I would like it to be for me to make a mountain out of a molehill and turn a perfectly peaceful moment into one oozing with drama.

Now, for the sake of simplicity, I will give you a great example of someone being selfish and creating discord where it need not be. That someone is me.

Before I dive into this story and lay my "literal" dirty laundry out for you to see, let me ask you a question. If you are engaged, married, dating or even divorced, does your significant other do something that drives you crazy? Something that you have asked countless times for them NOT to do and yet, the world keeps spinning and they keep driving you to desperation and insanity? Well, that is where this story begins.

Let me set the stage for you:

We had just moved into what was our "new" house. Determination to keep everything clean and nice was at an all-time high. Now let me say this, I am not the cleanest person in the world. I am usually some kind of dynamically cluttered mess. My husband, Joseph, knows this and still loves me. Yet, when we closed on our house and began moving in, something inside of me wanted to keep everything perfect. Why? For me, this house represented restoration of something that had been lost near a decade before.

> The problem with perfection is that it is unattainable.

The problem with perfection is that it is unattainable. We are not meant to be perfect. This is where unreasonable expectations are born. We go from expecting perfection from ourselves to expecting it of others. If you didn't have problems before, you sure will now! The enemy of our hearts and relationships sees opportunity calling and slams through the window of our peace like a wrecking ball!

About two months after moving in, I walked past my husband's socks for what felt like the hundredth time. They were sitting on the bedroom floor on his side of the bed. Our laundry hamper was six feet away in our closet. The doors leading there were all open so there were no obstacles in his way of putting them in their proper place. It was VERY obvious to me that he just didn't care about the house or keeping it clean. I was unreasonably furious. Hadn't I already asked him at least a dozen times to STOP LEAVING HIS SOCKS ON THE FLOOR.

Lord, forgive me for my impatience and anger!

My husband and I rarely fight about anything. Less than once a year we will have a heated disagreement. Here I was, creating conflict where none need exist. We had an argument of oversize proportions over dirty socks! When I look back at myself and my reaction combined with the disruption of peace in my marriage over something this insignificant, it makes me sad. That is time in my marriage that I can never get back and I let the enemy use me as a pawn of chaos.

No doubt, I can hear some of you wondering why my husband wouldn't just "do the right thing" and put his socks in the dirty clothes hamper. The answer is it simply wasn't something he thought was important. "It was just a couple socks" and he didn't understand my frustration at the lack of care about *how I felt!* Therein lies the problem. See, I thought our new house and all of its bells and whistles was just mine. Everyone needed to see how much this house meant to ME. Doesn't anyone care about taking care of this amazing house that God restored to us? I felt self-righteous about it to a point that I am ashamed of.

What was survival tip #1 again? Oh yeah, **It's not about me!**

While in my private Bible study a couple weeks later, the Holy Spirit convicted me and admonished me. When the Spirit was done, I felt thoroughly disciplined. *What do you mean?* Well, first God asked me a question.

If the socks are bothering YOU, why don't YOU put them in the hamper?

First off, I was not expecting to hear this question in my spirit. Lord knows I was probably avoiding thinking about that because I knew I was being petty. Before I could even answer, the next question came.

Are you fulfilling your calling as a Proverbs 31 wife when you berate your husband over socks?

At this prompt, I pulled out my Bible and looked up the verses in Proverbs pertaining to a godly wife. It's a long passage, but I pray you open your Bible up to Proverbs 31:10-31.

"A wife of noble character who can find? She is worth far more than rubies. Her husband has full confidence in her and lacks nothing of value. She brings him good, not harm, all the days of her life. She selects wool and flax and works with eager hands. She is like the merchant ships, bringing her food from afar. She gets up while it is still night; she provides food for her family and portions for her female servants. She considers a field and buys it; out of her earnings she plants a vineyard. She sets about her work vigorously; her arms are strong for her tasks. She sees that her trading is profitable, and her lamp does not go out at night. In her hand she holds the distaff and grasps the spindle with her fingers. She opens her arms to the poor and extends her hands to the needy. When it snows, she has no fear for her household; for all of them are clothed in scarlet. She makes coverings for her bed; she is clothed in fine linen and purple. Her husband is respected at the city gate, where he takes his seat among the elders of the land. She makes linen garments and sells them and supplies the merchants with sashes. She is clothed with strength and dignity; she can laugh at the days to come. She speaks with wisdom, and faithful instruction is on her tongue. She watches over the affairs of her household and does not eat the bread of idleness. Her children arise and call her blessed; her husband also, and he praises her: 'Many women do noble things, but you surpass them all.' Charm is deceptive,

and beauty is fleeting; but a woman who fears the LORD is to be praised. Honor her for all that her hands have done, and let her works bring her praise at the city gate." Proverbs 31:10-31

Let me be honest with you, I got to verse twelve and already felt like I had failed my husband. That is only three verses into the Bible's description of a worthy woman! *She brings him good, not harm, all the days of her life.* Here I was, fighting with my husband over socks! How was I honoring God and my husband by causing him harm over something so trivial?! I had taken the beauty of my marriage and reduced its value down to the cost of a pair of dirty socks.

Instead of the vindication I wanted for being right about how my husband should pick up his socks I was admonished. The last thing that came to mind was: *It's Not About You.*

Are you single?
Married and yet struggling?
Divorced?
Remarried?

God wants us to have a greater understanding of our role as a wife. His Word gives us a place to start when we stray from being the kind of wives that we have all been called to be.

I am sure you are all sitting at the edge of your seat, wondering what happened next in my great admonishment. Well, the unexpected happened. My perspective and mindset on how to be a Proverbs 31 wife changed. The selfish idea that the house was mine was replaced with the truth that my house belongs to God, and I am just a steward. My corrupted thoughts about my husband's disrespect of my requests to pick up his socks were replaced with what Christ taught us, servanthood.

Without telling him, I began picking up my husband's socks whenever I saw them on the floor. Much to my surprise, my anger and resentment were gone. (Praise the LORD!) I didn't see conflict sitting on my bedroom floor. Instead, I saw a way to better serve my husband. Jesus called us all to be servants.

"So the last will be first, and the first will be last."
(Matthew 20:16)

Do you know what happened next?

My husband began picking up his socks and putting them in the hamper! We don't give our partners enough credit for seeing us. Once he saw that it was important enough for me to take care of it for him, he began helping me with something that was now visibly important to me. We can claim something is important to us until the cows come home, but our actions have to match our words.

Marriage isn't about us. It's not about your spouse and it's not about you. It is about how we can take this holy union gifted to us by God and honor Him with it.

Carolyn and I are excited to bring you on this journey to Surviving Your Fairytale. The carriage is waiting, all you have to do is jump inside and let God take the reins.

Am I making
my marriage all
about me?

She comforts, encourages, and does him only
good and not evil all the days of her life.
~PROVERBS 31:12 AMP

Survival Tip #2

To truly be friends, one must be ready to seek another's interests over one's own.

A friend loves at all times...
~PROVERBS 17:17A

A re you getting ready to take the marital leap? Are you a seasoned spouse experienced in the ups and downs of marriage? Either way, we can all agree, saying "I do" is serious business. What you are really saying is, "Friend, I will lay down my life for you." *Are you truly ready to make such a commitment?* When we have just fallen head over heels in love, it can be hard to think about a life-or-death commitment. However, that is how God always intended for it to be.

The Proverbs verse that began this chapter in its entirety is *"A friend loves at all times, and a brother is born for adversity."* Interestingly the proverb is sandwiched between, *"Why should fools have money in hand to buy wisdom, when they are not able to understand it?"* (v. 16) and *"One who has no sense shakes hands in pledge and puts up security for a neighbor"* (v. 18).

Reading these words, it doesn't seem as though the primary author of Proverbs, King Solomon, was thinking about marriage. Although, with his hundreds of wives and concubines, one would think that is all he thought about! Despite Solomon's lady troubles, he was wise beyond measure. He knew a devoted friend would be more interested in the friendship itself than the things of this world. He must have known his share of adversity with those who would seek his friendship for their own selfish purposes. Marriage too can be for individual glory, but with a devoted friend, as it is with true love, *one must be ready to seek another's interests over one's own.* When you think about your fiancé, would you say he is your best friend?

I believe Solomon's intent in writing the majority of Proverbs was to help us understand the importance of having respect for God. Respecting God and His wisdom puts us on His path and gives your fairytale meaning and direction.

My son, if you accept my words and store up my commands within you, turning your ear to wisdom and applying your heart to understanding—indeed, if you call out for insight and cry aloud for understanding, and if you look for it as for silver and search for it as for hidden treasure, then you will understand the fear of the Lord *and find the knowledge of God. (Proverbs 2:1-5)*

Honestly, I've always been puzzled as to why Solomon allowed his seven hundred wives and three hundred concubines (who worshipped other gods, 1 Kings 11:3) to draw him away from the One True God. I seriously doubt he was friends with all his wives and concubines.

It's perhaps ironic or fitting that Proverbs ends with the Epilogue: The Wife of Noble Character which Tiarra expressed earlier. It was King Lemuel who wrote the Epilogue and who also learned from his mother, "Do not spend your strength on women, your vigor on those who ruin kings (Proverbs 31:3). Boy howdy (a favorite expression of Tiarra's) was she wise!

Let's think about one of the opening questions again. Are you truly ready to make such a commitment? When I think about this question, I'm reminded of one of the most beautiful verses of scripture offered by the beloved disciple, John.

Greater love has no one than this: to lay
down one's life for one's friends.
(John 15:13)

Let's pause for a minute and consider what laying down one's life could mean as it relates to marriage.

- Are you both on the same path in trying to understand and respect God?
- Are you willing to learn to show interest in (and even like) the things he likes to help build connection and companionship in your relationship?
- Will your love change if he gains weight or loses his hair?
- Will you still love him if he is paralyzed in an accident?
- Will you be his nurse if he has a lingering disease?
- Will you both agree to raise your children in the love of Christ?
- Will you seek help if you or your spouse develops an addiction of the flesh such as: alcohol, gambling, pornography?

If you answered no to even one of these questions, or hesitated, then stop! The Holy Spirit is telling you to seek the counsel of one of your trusted pastoral leaders. You may also want to consider a premarital course or some Christian counseling. Remember, you are not alone. Your fiancé may be uncertain too. Remember the opening proverb: "A *friend loves at ALL times."* Not just when you are having a good day, or when the intimacy is wonderful, or when he treats you like a princess. *The love for your best friend is always.*

My newly engaged sister in Christ, Liz, had been the victim of many poisonous experiences, so much so that marriage was not even on her mind.

Fear motivated my decision not to pursue relationships. I wasn't looking for a forever love. Having been hurt before, I realized it was better to be alone and place my life with God rather than to seek love. God had other plans. There were plenty of interested men, but I didn't share their interest. I just wasn't ready.

My best friend's brother lived in Texas and was relapsing. He came back home to find strength in being surrounded by family and friends. I heard he would be at our church camp that summer. Despite being at the same church, I still hadn't had the chance to meet him. It was heavy on my heart knowing that he was still struggling. One night, I was in prayer when I heard the Lord telling me to open my heart. It sounded like the scariest request. Even though I was afraid, I wanted to continue in being obedient, so I agreed.

I finally had a chance to meet him. It had been on my heart to share with him how much he was valued by everyone, especially God. I had taken a few psych classes so I thought I could help, but even more important than any help I could offer from what I had learned was helping him through my own walk with God. I had grown through so much trauma, and it was all because of my relationship with God. I wanted that for him. As we became friends, I shared my faith with him, and he started asking me questions about God. Before we knew it, we were growing closer, not only as friends, but later as a couple and in our walk with God together.

My fiancé grew up in a Christian home. Despite that, life and addiction drew him away from God. Thank goodness that no matter how far you go away from your calling and how much the devil thinks he has you, God's plan always prevails in the end. The last time he was struggling with breaking old habits, mindsets, and strongholds, I told him that the reason he should never stop pushing forward is the same reason I never gave up on him. I held onto God's promise. The promise that He can make all things new. The promise that He always forgives and the promise of who we are in Him. I held onto that promise and reminded him of who God says he is. NOW he does that for me. When I'm having a rough time, he reminds me who God says I am.

It's been such a privilege to see my fiancé not only come to Christ, but to see how he humbles himself before the Lord. He's a pretty tall guy, so when he worships with his hands raised high and you are sitting or standing in the back of the church, you know right away who's worshipping the Lord. Even though we haven't reached our wedding date, I have confidence in knowing he will be the spiritual leader for me always (and our children one day too). We are going through Christian premarital counseling and by the grace of God will be married by the time this book is in your hands. You know, when you hear God saying, "Trust Me," that's absolutely what you do.

Thank you, Liz, for showing the importance of understanding what it means to be a true friend to your spouse.

Had I been honest in answering questions like those above and been friends with my first husband, our marriage may not have ended in divorce. I must claim some responsibility for the failure as it was just the culmination of the consequences of a life lived without Christ. God clearly knows who we will choose as our mates and even the "frogs" in the forest of our lives. You know the expression, "You have to kiss a lot of frogs before you find your prince"? Well, God allows them on our path for His reasons. And yet, God NEVER advocates divorce. He wants the best for you both.

Jesus replied, "Moses permitted you to divorce
your wives because your hearts were hard. But it was
not this way from the beginning. I tell you that anyone
who divorces his wife, except for sexual immorality,
and marries another woman commits adultery."
(Matthew 19:8-9)

God also does not advocate the abuse and breaking down of His children. If the fires of your marriage have dwindled and you think they could be kindled elsewhere, Tiarra and I encourage you to seek pastoral counseling. That said, if you are in an abusive relationship and find yourself in an unsafe situation, seek help right away. Don't wait thinking that it will get better.

That said, divorce should be your last resort. Seek guidance from pastors in your church if you are contemplating divorce. Marriage is a gift from God. He has given you a best friend to "do" life with; do it for His glory.

My parents' marriage regrettably suffered from a good deal of disappointment. My mother had several miscarriages, putting a strain on the relationship and adding pain to their life. This fact, accompanied by my father's horrific experiences as a prisoner of war in Nazi Germany during World War II, made for a very troubled marriage. I'm not certain they were ever friends.

Shortly after Bob and I were married, I was a psychology major studying two thousand years of musings from philosophers like Aristotle, Plato, and Socrates, to humanists like Kurt Vonnegut and nihilists like Frederick Nietzsche. As daft as he was, even Nietzsche knew "It's not a lack of love but a lack of friendship that makes unhappy marriages." [3]

There was a time in my forest when I didn't feel much like Cinderella, but wished I was Rapunzel. Locked in a second-story bedroom by one of the frogs, I was only let out when it was time for work or when I was "needed." How I ached for long, long hair! Take this to heart: God doesn't want any one of His precious children hurt, ever. We can't blame God for the choices we make, especially when things turn bad or the frogs in our life get nasty and mean. Again though, flee an abusive relationship as God doesn't want anyone hurt!

> Glory for God comes when we show the world that it is His Grace and Grit that allows us to survive.

Life is hard. Bad things happen and most of the time we won't understand why. *Bad things still happen to the Lord's people.* When you are in Christ you can be sure that the enemy will target you and your marriage. Glory for God comes when we show the world that it is His Grace and Grit that allows us to survive. The evil one will do everything he can to discourage you and veer you off God's path, especially when your fairytale takes a tumble in the forest. Let me be clear though as I speak from experience. Surviving your marriage should not mean a physical survival. It means that in your marriage there will be challenges of all proportions and it will take the two of you turning to God to work through those challenges. This inspirational guide is meant to help you in being a better helpmate for him. He in turn will prayerfully respond with love. Jesus instructs, *"Husbands, love your wives, just as Christ loved the church and gave himself up for her..."* (Ephesians 5:25).

Nowhere in the Bible does it say, if you choose Jesus, you will have a perfect life or even the fairytale you think you deserve. Keep in mind the example you set of how you treat each other in your marriage is on display for all to see. When you are living out loud and sharing how God has helped you overcome challenges in your marriage, not only will you honor God, but others will see so much is possible when you depend on HIM. In this way you may be helping achieve God's purpose for you. That purpose is to not only accept Him as Savior and King but to bring as many people as possible with us into His Kingdom. On this journey to Him we want to help you realize not only your purpose in Him but the plans He has for you.

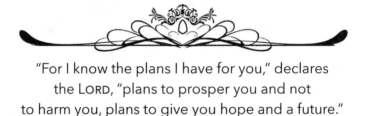

"For I know the plans I have for you," declares
the LORD, "plans to prosper you and not
to harm you, plans to give you hope and a future."
(Jeremiah 29:11)

Speaking of hope and a future, I turn to my precious Bob. He is my best friend. Our friendship flourished when I went to work at the same company where he worked. There were those who questioned our friendship, including our parents. I suspect what caught everyone off guard was our age difference. He was in his fifties and I in my early thirties. People asked, *What could they have in common?* At the time, the answer was … sports! We loved to talk and watch all sports, especially baseball. Today, it seems all the sports leagues and many players have gone "woke" so we've tuned out, but back in the early 1990s we were fanatical.

Bob was an amazing athlete. In fact, he was an All-American golfer at Stanford University. He always bristles when I brag on him, saying, "Don't tell people that, it was two hundred years ago." Whenever he says that it reminds me of one of our founding fathers and his wife. Their love story is one that turned heads for sure. John Adams was our first vice president and second president. He and his wife, Abigail, had an amazing friendship and love story which is well chronicled through their letters. John Adams had copies of the letters made. Remember, they didn't have a copy machine or Office Max; their letters were handwritten. He knew their friendship/love would be a standard-bearer for history geeks like me.

According to historian and biographer Joseph J. Ellis, "One of the distinctive features of their extraordinary correspondence over a lifetime—more than twelve hundred letters—was also present from the start, namely, the tendency to banter playfully about serious subjects, thereby creating a certain ambiguity as to whether the issue at stake was cause for concern or laughter." [4]

When I recall how people seemed concerned about our age difference, I wanted to say... Hey, Abigail was fifteen and John was twenty-four! [5] Ellis wrote, "There were so many topics they could talk about easily and just as many things they did not have to talk about at all." [6] Yep, that's us too!

Can you say that about your fiancé?

The candor they shared is nothing short of refreshing and essential for a healthy marriage. If you can't be honest early on, it will only become harder if not impossible later.

An honest answer is like a kiss on the lips.
(Proverbs 24:26)

Just prior to their wedding, Abigail asked John a question and I wonder if she was expecting such honesty? She asked, "'... tell me all my faults, both of omission and commission, and all the evil you either know or think of me.' John responded with a mock 'catalogue of your Faults, Imperfections, Deficits, or whatever you please to call them.' She was, he observed, negligent at playing cards, could not sing a note, often hung her head like a bulrush, sat with her legs crossed, was pigeon-toed, and to cap it off, she read too much." [7]

Read too much? That would have stopped me in my tracks from the man. Her response was one that sets the standard for their continued playful banter and honesty. "… many of these defects were incurable, especially the reading, so he would have to learn to live with them. The leg-crossing charge struck her as awkward, since a 'gentleman has no business to concern himself with the leggs of a lady.'" [8]

It's not likely they spoke to each other in this manner when they were together as "letter writing in the eighteenth century was a more deliberative and self-consciously artful exercise."[9] Regardless, the point here is brutal honesty ahead of time will save a good deal of heartache and even save you from making a terrible, life-altering mistake.

Speaking of life-altering—scratch that—world-altering mistake, let's consider Eve.

When the woman saw that the fruit of the tree was good
for food and pleasing to the eye, and also desirable for
gaining wisdom, she took some and ate it. She also gave
some to her husband, who was with her, and he ate it.
(Genesis 3:6)

Ever since the Fall, the evil one's venom has been present in this world. God's people have too often chosen snake venom to control the lives we lead. We must seek God's Grace and Grit to withstand the venom. We must remember He wants us to choose Life. He wants us to choose Love, or Life **O**ver **V**enom **E**veryday.

♛

It is time for a strange and yet critically important question. Are you and your fiancé/spouse friends? The fairytales we know and love never showed us courtship and we really never saw friendship before those movies rolled the credits. Now, before we can answer that, I need to ask you another question. Are you ready to carry all the baggage that comes with your soon-to-be spouse? If you are already married, then I ask you, how are you doing carrying all the baggage that comes with a marital partnership?

Everyone Has Baggage

If you talk to any of your friends, whether they are male or female, I am sure you have heard stories of different life events they have survived. Friendship is where we tend to feel more comfortable in sharing those deep dark life moments and familiar insecurities that we all have in common. Why is it when we begin dating someone (without the prerequisite of friendship) do we sweep all the things that made us who we are under the rug, with the hope they are never seen again? They can't see you without makeup and they don't need to know anything about your troubled teen years. After we get married, then we can start letting things out slowly. We don't want to scare them off! We talk less about the things that are most important before joining our lives with someone else.

Hear me out, I am absolutely no different. In fact, I recently began working through the AA 12-step program. Now let me frame that with the fact that I am not an alcoholic, nor do I struggle with drug addiction. Instead, I had been struggling with trauma caused by some very dark times in my life and I no longer wanted to be held captive by those moments. My pastor once told me, "Anyone can work the 12

steps." One day during yet another epic meltdown over my many fail-
ures, I decided it was time to work the 12 steps. Not only did I deserve
freedom, but everyone who loved me didn't deserve the spillover from
my baggage.

Walking through your own life with
open eyes and perfect 20/20 vision of the
experiences that are long past, you may find
yourself with an ability to figure out what
serves you and what does not. I learned that
I had been carrying around a twelve-piece
luggage set of rejection. My addiction to re-
jection affected my husband and my children and my life as a whole.
It touched every relationship that I had. When you get engaged or if
you're already married you will find you are part of something that is
much bigger than you. You are agreeing to take on all of someone else's
trauma and relationship statuses and most times that can be really hard.

**It is not your job
to fix your spouse.**

Marriage isn't just the fancy dress and changed social media status.
When you get married, you are promising to carry that burden with
your spouse—no matter what it is, and whether you know it is there or
not.

Let me stop you before you decide your fiancé (or husband, if you are
married) is a project you can fix. This isn't about changing your spouse
or even helping him through his own baggage. That is his job and God's
job. All trying to fix someone else will do for you is create even greater
discord in those relationships. Instead, this is an opportunity for us to
explore the baggage that we have and to determine what things we can
let go of. The less we carry from the past, the better partner we can be
and the better able we are to help our husbands carry their burdens.
I want you to remember something that is very important. It is not
your job to fix your spouse. Your only job is to love him, accept him,
support him, and work together to create a life that serves God, your

relationship, and creates a lasting impact on those who witness your lives together.

Now, before you hire a divorce attorney or call your best friend to break up with your fiancé (because this all sounds too hard), let me share a story with you about friendship and why that building block can help you traverse all of the trauma this world has to offer (and trust me, it offers a lot!). It took not one marriage, but two for me to learn just how important it is to start things off as friends. Oy, I can hear you objecting already, "Is this lady giving us marriage and relationship advice and she has been divorced?" Yes, yes, I am, and guess what? I am very qualified. Why? I have been through a lot and still God makes me new every day. What better way for you to avoid mistakes and pitfalls than to learn from someone who fell out of the relationship tree and hit every branch on the way down?

My first marriage started off as the rose-colored glasses parade. Two heavily traumatized individuals moving in together, moving across the States, and then getting married because my then boyfriend said, "Our choices are you move out or we get married. Want to get married?" Isn't that just the most romantic proposal you ever heard? I must have been color-blind to miss the giant red flag waving in front of me. Since we were never friends, I truly feel it was all he was capable of. There is a kinship that is missing from any relationship if you can't be friends. It is as if there is a barrier to being completely honest.

It was obvious through so many aspects of our marriage. Growing up, the only thing I ever wanted to be was a wife and mother. Instead, my spouse didn't share much in common with me and I spent a lot of time trying to teach myself to love what he loved. Isn't that what a good wife does? Even if it was what a good wife does, all I ever heard was how I was failing at it.

I didn't leave my marriage because I was unhappy. I left in fear. Emotionally abused for fourteen years and with the scales lifted from my eyes, I wondered if my girls and I would make it from one day to the next. It was an experience that left me with a lot of unresolved trauma. I brought that trauma with me everywhere I went, and it affected every relationship that I had. I buried it low and didn't work to learn from what had happened. I didn't take time to move past the trauma, forgive and let go of everything that had happened and give it all back to God. I thought the way to get friends and build relationships was through self-sacrifice and sabotage. I was always seeking to make others feel better even if warming their hands meant setting myself on fire.

When I met my second husband, Joseph, we were both working at Starbucks. I was newly divorced, and he had just moved back in with his parents to go back to school. Ideal for a potential mate, eh? Before he and I were anything romantic, we were friends. We talked about life, and about the things we had experienced long before we ever became a couple. Hopes and dreams, hurts, losses, and beliefs. I truly believe that many of those late-night conversations built between us a bridge through which to support each other through the trauma we each brought into our eventual courtship and later marriage. Joseph has helped me become the Proverbs 31 wife that I always prayed I would be. His friendship is even more invaluable to me now and I look back and I can only see how God made roads to lead me here.

Let me be frank with you: everyone has some kind of trauma. It doesn't matter if you grew up in the perfect family and the perfect town. Everyone is going to have something that happened to them that they push down and hide away. Without us knowing, it carries over into everything we do. Happily Ever After is something that is absolutely attainable. It is something that you work for, something you pray for, and something that you sacrifice for. At the end of the day, it takes two people to build it, and a dependence on the God of Abraham, Isaac, and Jacob. As you prepare to walk through this journey of learning more about how you can be a faithful, loving, and Christlike spouse, I want you to keep your mind open to finding those burdens that you have been carrying for way too long. It's time to lay them at the foot of the cross.

Mirror Mirror on the Wall ...

Am I a true
friend to my
spouse?

A friend loves at all times...
~PROVERBS 17:17A

Survival Tip #3

To love God and each other is to truly live and it's your choice to make.

I am the way and the truth and the life.

~JOHN 14:6

*I*t is so easy to feel lost. All of us have felt as though we are floating on the ocean, missing our sail, no rudder to provide direction. The opening scripture was the answer Jesus gave to doubting Thomas when he asked, *"Lord, we don't know where you are going, so how can we know the way?" (John 14:5).*

Have you asked God the same thing a time or two? Some of you may wrestle with this question over the decision regarding marriage. Maybe if you are divorced you are now looking for clarity and direction for your life. When Jesus says He is "life," what does that mean? To get that answer, we need to go back to a decision in the Garden of Eden that would change everything.

The LORD God took the man and put him in the Garden of Eden to work it and take care of it. And the LORD God commanded the man, "You are free to eat from any tree in the garden; but you must not eat from the tree of the knowledge of good and evil, for when you eat from it you will certainly die." (Genesis 2:15-17)

Eve's fateful decision, and Adam's acceptance of that decision, brought sin and spiritual death to all humanity. We were separated from God and left with no prospect for a life of love with Him. Adam and Eve made a choice.

And the LORD God said, "The man has now become like one of us, knowing good and evil. He must not be allowed to reach out his hand and take also from the tree of life and eat, and live forever." (Genesis 3:22)

What is the tree of life and why wouldn't God want us to live forever? For those answers we need to briefly consider the Seforitic tree, or what we Christians call Jacob's Ladder.

According to Elizabeth Oakley, my professor at Colorado Theological Seminary, the Seforitic tree is considered the ten attributes of God that we perfect within ourselves as we climb higher toward God. Each attribute of God is considered a limb of the tree. [10]

Jacob interpreted the tree of life in the form of a stairway to heaven. The idea of ascending each rung suggests gaining greater insight into His Shekinah Glory. One website, Compelling Truth, defines Shekinah Glory in this way: "The Shekinah Glory is the Hebrew name given to the presence of God dwelling on earth." [11]

He had a dream in which he saw a stairway resting on the earth, with its top reaching to heaven, and the angels of God were ascending and descending on it. There above it stood the LORD, and he

*said: "I am the L**ORD**, the God of your father Abraham and the God*
of Isaac. I will give you and your descendants the land on which
you are lying. Your descendants will be like the dust of the earth,
and you will spread out to the west and to the east, to the north and
to the south. All peoples on earth will be blessed through you and
your offspring. I am with you and will watch over you wherever
you go, and I will bring you back to this land. I will not leave you
until I have done what I have promised you."
(Genesis 28:12-15)

Without getting too deep into Jewish law or allowing the false teaching of Gnosticism to creep in, I will simply offer this explanation as found on Christianity.com: "The tree of life, first referenced in the book of Genesis, is a life-giving tree created to support the physical and spiritual life of mankind." [12] But when Adam and Eve violated God's command, they immediately became separated from Him. He had no other choice but to take away their ability to continue to eat from the tree of life.

In the book of Revelation, the tree of life is a symbol of Christ.

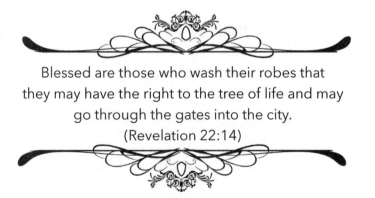

Blessed are those who wash their robes that
they may have the right to the tree of life and may
go through the gates into the city.
(Revelation 22:14)

This truth shows us if we want to be redeemed to God, we must confess our sin with all our heart. We then become reborn into the life that Christ and His Father are anxious for us to have, an eternal fairytale lived in the glory and grace of our Creator, as He originally intended.

Jesus, to those of us who choose Him, becomes our life-giving tree.

Another website, GotQuestions.org, offers this explanation for why God kept the first man and woman from the tree of life:

> "It was a mercy that God kept us from the tree of life. By barring access to the tree of life, God showed compassion in His Omniscience. Knowing that, because of sin, earthly life would be filled with sorrow and toil, God graciously limited the number of years men would live. To live eternally in a sinful state would mean endless agony for humanity, with no hope of the relief that comes with death. By limiting our lifespan, God gives us enough time to come to know Him and His provision for eternal life through Christ but spares us the misery of an endless existence in a sinful condition." [13]

That's why our lives are limited. Let's live our brief lives here with purpose for Him as He loved us first. Let's always choose love (**L**ife **O**ver **V**enom **E**veryday). Jesus reminds us of the importance of loving God and each other, adding, *"There is no commandment greater than these"* (Mark 12:31).

It's important not to be confused about His comment relative to a "commandment." The actual words, *"Love the LORD your God with all your heart and with all your soul and with all your strength"* (Deuteronomy 6:5) are not among the Ten Commandments. These words were offered by Moses to the assembly as part of what is referred to in Jewish law as the "Shema," recited every morning and evening by Orthodox Jews.

Why wouldn't God make loving Him one of the Ten Commandments? Because He gave us free will to love Him and others. He didn't want to force Himself on us. He wants us to keep the commandments and decrees and to fear (respect) Him so *"that we might always prosper and be kept alive"* (Deuteronomy 6:24). The reference to *kept alive* certainly could be literal, given the might of our

Almighty God, but it tells us of a Creator who loves His creation so deeply that He wants us to always choose the life He gives us which is love.

He wants it so much for us that the last and newest "command" of loving one another (John 13:34) is what He leaves us with shortly before He would be crucified. FOR US!

It's no accident the word "live" spelled backwards is "evil;" it's your choice. *To love God and each other is to live and it's your choice.*

Think of it. The only thing God wants from you is your love. Why should that be so difficult? Why do we rebel? Why do we resist His love? Especially when our capacity to love comes from Him. *"We love because he first loved us"* (1 John 4:19).

A life respecting Him, accepting His Son as our Way, our Truth, and our Life, respecting our spouses and choosing love daily – now that's a fairytale come true.

God loved Adam. He created Adam and only wanted what was best for him. Instead, Adam chose venom, just as I did before God came after me.

A life respecting Him, accepting His Son as our Way, our Truth, and our Life, respecting our spouses and choosing love daily – now that's a fairytale come true. Tiarra and I pray that if you absorb nothing else from this guide that you will let the truth of the prior sentence glide into your heart as easily as that glass slipper fits your precious foot!

Carolyn and I have discussed each section at length to determine how best to serve each of you who picks up this book. This survival tip about love comes with an anecdote from me. As you read each word, I pray the Holy Spirit shows you great love and you see why Jesus made love the greatest commandment.

Do you sometimes wonder if you are important to God? When I was praying for my marriage to be fixed, I felt like He was silent, and I wondered if He was still out there, still creating miracles, still showing up. The truth is, He is always there. Sometimes it is His silence that speaks the loudest. When we want answers, we stand around staring at the sky waiting for a miracle. That is exactly what I was waiting for. Then, a month before I moved out on my own with my daughters a song came on the radio. It's called "Grey Street" by Dave Matthews. I am sure that shows my age but stay with me. See, part of the lyrics speak of a girl who prays to a God she doesn't believe exists (though she hopes He does) and she asks if she is supposed to take it on herself to get out of the place she's in. (Sound familiar?) I asked God to move a mountain for me. What I didn't expect was to wake up next to a shovel. Sometimes the miracle is simply us making a decision. This wasn't the mountain I originally wanted moved, but now that I stood before it, I realized, if I wanted a mountain moved, I was going to have to start digging. Why? This mountain was what stood between me and my happily ever after. It had to go!

As I dug up that mountain and ventured off into single-mom land, (sporting three daughters and an ex-husband as my carry-on luggage for this new life I was forging), I realized that dating had to be something created by Satan. It seemed engineered to help us feel like each new attempt to find that "special" someone was met with Mr. Not-Right-Now and sometimes even worse, Mr. Wrong. Oh, to be loved. To be accepted as we are, no strings attached, no change required. After a tumultuous marriage, all I longed for was someone to see me and say, "That's my girl. She is perfect for me just the way she is." Isn't that what we all long for in our own happily ever after?

Dating is hard. Not only is it hard when you are in your youthful twenties looking for who you want to navigate this life with but imagine being out of the dating scene for over fourteen years! Like me, you may find yourself wondering how you are supposed to find Mr. Right. For me I wondered how I was going to find him since I had obviously not found him the first time. I hated dating even before I got divorced. My dream was to grow up and be a wife and mom. Now, looking over that first year of being single, I can see the desperation in me to find someone to fill that gaping void left behind by my first marriage.

As year two of single motherhood began, I walked into it with silent determination. I would stay single and be alone with God. I wanted to understand my relationship with God better, and I knew that if I was ever going to be ready to be someone's wife again, I better first learn to depend only on Him. When you finally give things over to God, you would be amazed at what happens. Barely into that year, I met Joseph (my love) while I was working as a barista at Starbucks. My first impression of this twitchy, anxious-looking guy was pretty minimal. He was handsome, but it didn't occur to me to think of him in any way other than as someone I worked with.

Despite me starting off with Joseph in the friendzone, he was like warm rays of sunshine in the dead of winter, and we became fast friends. As I started to make more friends at my job, I realized it was crazy that I had never had friends to just have fun with, sans kids. My eyes were opening up to a world where what I needed mattered too. With Joseph, I was learning you could spend time with someone and just goof off and not put on make-up or try to like what they like. No need to fake anything. Just two friends hanging out.

Love is a tricky thing. The more time I spent with Joseph, the more I began to realize that he was kind of perfect for me. He didn't care for sports, loved video games, loved cartoons and comic books. I even told him that I thought he must be an alien. Guys like him just weren't real in this world. Despite my romantic thoughts beginning to shift, I was still very much in the mode of "not doing anything with my dating life until God does something." I wasn't going to make a single move.

After spending nearly every evening together for a week, I said goodbye to him one night and closed the door after him. Almost instantly I received a text message from him. It took my breath away. It said:

"In another life, you would have been perfect for me."

I can't tell you how long I stared at my phone screen with my back leaned against my apartment door. In my mind, I pictured him just on the other side. It still seemed as though he was a world away. Everything flowed from that moment. He saw me at all moments. From good to bad and everything in between. He stayed for all of them. He got to know the real me and I got to know the real him. It was the most freedom in building a relationship that I had ever experienced. Funny enough, it was also the easiest thing in the world.

Love is just accepting someone exactly as they are, requiring nothing and YET gaining everything together.

When it came time for him to meet my family, my middle daughter decided that it would be a good time to fall in the creek at the park and split her head open. She came screaming out of the creek looking like Carrie from Stephen King! I had no ride, so Joseph offered to take us to the ER to get her stapled up. On the way there, she threw up in the back seat of his car. I was mortified. Here I was, trying to impress him and my family at this outing and there had already been blood and vomit. I was sure I would never see him again.

Love is so much bigger and so much easier than we think it is. We overcomplicate it and add conditions and stipulations upon something that was intended to be fully and freely given, seeking nothing in return. See, love is just accepting someone exactly as they are, requiring nothing and YET gaining everything together. Your success in any relationship is based on how well you love. Your marriage will thrive if you love above all else and follow the advice in the book of James for the rest:

Understand this, my beloved brothers and sisters. Let everyone be quick to hear [be a careful, thoughtful listener], slow to speak [a speaker of carefully chosen words and], slow to anger [patient, reflective, forgiving]; for the [resentful, deep-seated] anger of man does not produce the righteousness of God [that standard of behavior which He requires from us].
(James 1:19-20 AMP)

There are a million memories I could share with you cataloguing how God showed me I could be loved by someone who is just as human as I am. If you are engaged reading this, you get to choose to keep your relationship as fresh and exciting as the day you first kissed. If you are married and you feel that the coals in the fire have been cooling down, you have the power to reignite them! It all comes from love!

Let me tell you, friend, the reality of marriage is that it is hard work. I can hear you telling me, "No kidding, this girl must be Nancy Drew puzzling out this mystery of marriage." I know that isn't news, but the real news is that it isn't hard for the reason you think. It is not just because you are choosing to stay with someone forever and now you have to figure out what to eat for dinner until you both die. Instead, it is hard because you must show up, every day, no matter what. Being a human is messy! You and your husband will have to show up every single day, especially when life is chaos. Being in the darker moments and still being there, in love, with your husband. That is what is hard. When you get married, you are agreeing to love someone else in their mess. It is also allowing them to love you in yours.

Love is where you start, mercy and grace are where you live. Joseph did come back after that fun family day at the park. His things slowly migrated to my apartment. On one such night, when the two of us both had work and school early in the morning, everything changed. See, I had to be at work at 4:00 a.m., and Joseph had class at 8:00 a.m. It was midnight, and we continued laughing at funny videos on the

Love is where you start, mercy and grace are where you live.

internet, not wanting our evening to end. We knew we both needed sleep, but we had reached a point where we wanted to always be in each other's space. As I got up to say our goodnights, Joseph grabbed my hand, looked me in the eyes and said words I will never forget. *"I don't want to go."* I replied with, *"Then don't."* In that moment, we were inseparable.

Our unconventional beginnings had a gift imbedded within them from God. Joseph and I both learned how to be ourselves, fully and freely. To be part of something that didn't come with relationship obligations. Instead, we were just there, loving each other's company and learning about each other along the way.

Jesus gave us the example of love. He gave us the greatest commandment to love others as we love ourselves. As you prepare to walk down the aisle, rededicate your marriage, or even refresh the current marriage chapter that God is writing through you, remember that love truly can be enough.

Do I truly love
God and His
people?

"A new command I give you: Love one another. As I have loved you,
so you must love one another. By this everyone will know that you
are my disciples, if you love one another."
~JOHN 13:34-35

Survival Tip #4

A joyful life means finding our purpose in Him.

Let us rejoice and be glad and give him glory! For the wedding of the Lamb has come, and his bride has made herself ready.
~REVELATION 19:7

*O*nce upon a time in the forests of Big Sur, California, a fairytale was unfolding. The night air was dense with calm amid a looming presence of a once-in-a-lifetime joy. There wasn't a hint of the characteristic fog, rain, or wind that typically envelops the wintry California coast. It was perfection on earth. It was 6:00 p.m. on January 15, 1994.

Bob and I were enjoying a winter getaway at a secluded mountain resort overlooking the Pacific Ocean. Earlier in the day we roamed the streets of Carmel-by-the-Sea, a quaint shopping haven laden with small boutiques and local artisan treasures.

We had settled into our cozy cottage and were preparing for a short walk to a romantic dinner. The restaurant was at the end of a winding, unpaved, and forested path. A bottle of perfectly chilled Perrier Jouet champagne sat nestled in a bucket of ice next to a roaring fire.

As I laced up my hiking boots for the walk ahead, Bob knelt on one knee, took my hand in his, looked into my eyes, and uttered those four beautiful words. Will you marry me?

I felt like Cinderella—well, with hiking boots instead of glass slippers!

A joyful life means finding our purpose in Him.

Looking at the loving face of my soon-to-be husband, I felt my heart pounding like a crashing wave, my smile was as wide as the Pacific Ocean. Prince Charming just asked me to marry him. I could hear an exuberant and breathless, "Yes, yes!" coming out of my mouth but kisses soon replaced words.

God wrote in the romantic Song of Songs, *"Let him kiss me with the kisses of his mouth—for your love is more delightful than wine"* (Song of Songs 1:2). My passion for this man truly knows no bounds.

As he slipped the eye-popping diamond ring on my shaking left hand, it fit perfectly. What joy! Neither of us at that time understood the saving love of Jesus Christ. Perhaps you figured that out already as we had escaped to a mountain retreat and spent many a night enjoying the fruit of the vine.

In that beautiful moment of our happy engagement, how could we truly know the joy God had purposed for us? *A joyful life means finding our purpose in Him.*

And we know that in all things God works for the good of those who love him, who have been called according to his purpose.
(Romans 8:28)

God knew what our fairytale held for His glory and equipped us with His grit for His purpose.

Author Hayley DiMarco in her book *The Fruitful Wife* shares that the "lack of fruit in our lives doesn't speak to our sad state and our miserable or mediocre life, but to a failure to grasp our purpose here on earth" [14]

Bob's unconditional love has made being joyful easy. The day I said, "I will" was the happiest day of my life. We married in Kona, Hawaii. I bought my dress in a local shop. I wanted Bob to go with me to see if he liked it … which he did. No superstitions here!

By this time, I made three wonderful friends who brought their husbands and children with them to Hawaii. Until Bob, I never imagined I would know such joy. He has such an easy countenance, not only with me but with everyone—today, he even makes his caregivers smile.

There were, regrettably, those who offered a "Good luck; you know you will probably be his nurse his whole life." I allowed their hurtful comments to affect my joy.

"Joy robbers" is a phrase coined by my doctoral professor, Dr. Elizabeth Oakley. She said there are five "joy robbers."

1. Unconfessed sin

2. Unrestrained tongue

3. Neglected spiritual life

4. Unresolved doubt

5. Circumstances controlling us

Joy robbers had "robbed me blind" for the first thirty-three years of my life, but so had I. When I read Pastor Warren's book, the scales fell off my eyes with those four words, "It's not about you." [15]

I keep asking that the God of our Lord Jesus Christ, the glorious Father, may give you the Spirit of wisdom and revelation, so that you may know him better. I pray that the eyes of your heart may be enlightened in order that you may know the hope to which he has called you, the riches of his glorious inheritance in his holy people, and his incomparably great power for us who believe. That power is the same as the mighty strength he exerted when he raised Christ from the dead and seated him at his right hand in the heavenly realms, far above all rule and authority, power and dominion, and every name that is invoked, not only in the present age but also in the one to come. And God placed all things under his feet and appointed him to be head over everything for the church, which is his body, the fullness of him who fills everything in every way. (Ephesians 1:17-23)

How perfectly and beautifully expressed by the apostle Paul. We should pray this prayer for all who are lacking joy. Hayley DiMarco puts it this way:

"Joy comes when you realize that your life is never, for one second, a surprise to God. He hasn't lost all control, and things aren't happening willy-nilly. When you become mindful of the concept of God's complete and total sovereignty in your life, you can find joy in every situation." [16]

However, we must be aware of an important fact.

"Joy can coexist with sorrow and suffering, whereas sorrow without joy is a tyrannical emotion that snuffs out hope and faith." [17]

Gosh, I wish I had said that!

When Bob, now in his diseased state, says, "That attack was almost unbearable," it's difficult to find joy in sorrow. We hang onto the apostle Paul's words:

For our struggle is not against flesh and blood,
but against the rulers, against the authorities,
against the powers of this dark world and against
the spiritual forces of evil in the heavenly realms.
(Ephesians 6:12)

I recently read an online article in Vogue.com on March 7, 2022, that proves how joy can coexist with sorrow. The long and short of this story is that a Ukrainian couple planning their wedding prior to the Russian invasion found themselves instead planning to take up arms for their country. Despite the horrors and sorrows of war surrounding them, they traded their gown and tux for camouflage and were married on the battlefield.

Following the ceremony the bride declared, "I'm happy that we are alive, that this day started, that my husband is alive, and he is with me." After the ceremony, they held a small reception complete with a champagne toast and wedding cake. [18] I don't know about you but that's about all the simultaneous joy and sorrow that I can handle!

Of the joy robbers, pick one of the five that robs you from your fairytale. Write how you will put the robber in handcuffs!

- Unconfessed sin

- Unrestrained tongue

- Neglected spiritual life

- Unresolved doubt

- Circumstances controlling us

Now that the joy robbers are behind bars, Tiarra and I pray you will choose to be **J**ubilant **O**ver **Y**ahweh…. The Great I Am!

The Thief of Joy

When Carolyn asked me to help her write this book, I humbly accepted. It has never been hard for me to share my journey with Joseph because God breathed new life into me through every moment we have had. Joseph is the easiest part of my life and if I am running low on joy, it is probably my own fault.

Wouldn't it be just dandy if we could blame all of our stolen moments of joy on others?

The unfortunate truth is this: Something that lives inside of us cannot be stolen without our permission. The enemy likes to ruin our day and we let him do it with the simplest of things. Ever had your morning start off bad and it just spread like a plague through the entire day? Maybe your car didn't start. Perhaps you found out you didn't get the big promotion. Maybe your neighborhood barista messed up your coffee. I mean, that is a serious offense!

Imagine with me for a second that you have $5,000. Now, let's say I take $500 from you, and then I burn it. Would you take the remaining $4,500 and throw it in my little money bonfire? Of course not! Then why do we all let five minutes steamroll an entire day? My mom once asked me, "Did you have a bad day, or did you have a bad few minutes that you milked all day?" We have more power than we know to take back our day, but Satan doesn't want you to know that. He wants you to think that nothing good will happen for the rest of the day. If we settle on that way of thinking, that is exactly what will happen. We can also allow a single moment to taint future moments because of hurt we harbor inside.

Raise your hand if you are guilty of allowing the enemy to steal many moments of joy because of one moment that someone else hurt you. (You can't see me, but I have my hand raised.) For instance, consider my first Christmas with Joseph. My life was so full of joy being with him that our first Christmas together was looking to be magical. There was even snow in the forecast—in Texas! There was just one catch. Joseph's parents didn't want him to bring home his girlfriend for the holiday. When Christmas morning arrived, Joseph and I and the girls (who had become like his own daughters to him) all opened presents together and enjoyed our little family moment. Then he went to his parents' home without me.

To make my heart even sadder, it was time for the girls to go to their biological dad's house. As I stood with

Each one of us is the worst stealer of joy. my arms wrapped around my shoulders, bracing against the strange Texas weather, I watched my heart drive away in two cars while the magical snow was falling all around me. My joy drove away with those cars. I was just a mess the rest of the day!

What is worse, I held onto that moment for nearly a decade. Every holiday was just a little gray as I hung on to the false belief that I wasn't good enough for them.

Carolyn's list of joy-stealing offenders is spot on. The only thing it is missing is you. Don't take it personally; I steal my own joy very literally every day. I have to choose to take it back. See, each one of us is the worst stealer of joy. Whether it is because we believe that sorrow and joy don't share the same space, or if it is simply because we "want to be mad" right now. We are more often than not the reason that we lack joy. The other reason we can lack joy is that we simply expect others, especially our spouses, to provide that joy for us. I don't know if you know this, but I will let you in on a little secret. Are you ready?

It is NOT your spouse's job to make you happy or joyful! You might want to read that again. Our joy should be in the Lord. Your spouse is there to be a partner and someone who helps you travel the road of life. They didn't sign up to be your personal clown or your daily dose of perfect inspiration. We must be able to find joy and happiness in life so that anything that our husband brings is simply icing on the cake! Did I mention that joy-in-the-Lord cake has zero calories?

Joy is a gift from God. We get to choose how and when we will have it simply by giving our day-to-day moments over to God. All the good ones and the bad ones too. Nothing you have going on in your life or your marriage is too big for God. I didn't know if my in-laws would ever accept me and my girls. I learned I didn't need to know. Joseph had taken us in as his own. He required nothing but our love in return. It took longer than I care to admit for me to realize that I had stolen my own precious moments away wondering if someone was going to accept me.

If this is you, let me tell you something that I have to remind myself of daily. You are loved by an Almighty God. You are the daughter of the Most High King! You are royalty, love. Remember that no one can make you feel small if you don't let them. Stop letting the person that steals your joy away be you!

Mirror Mirror on the Wall ...

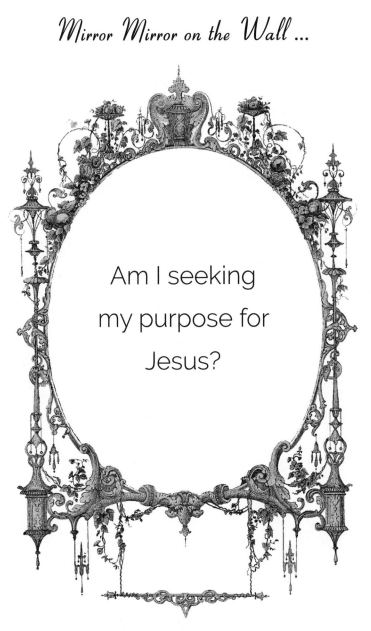

Am I seeking
my purpose for
Jesus?

"For I know the plans I have for you," declares the LORD,
"plans to prosper you and not to harm you,
plans to give you hope and a future."
~JEREMIAH 29:11

Survival Tip #5

Don't expect to find His peace if you don't find time for Him.

I have told you these things, so that in me you may
have peace. In this world you will have trouble.
But take heart! I have overcome the world.

~JOHN 16:33

*S*HALOM! This Hebrew word for peace is an all-encompassing blessing. The very book you are reading now is a collection of stories that have been shared to help you take these lessons and pass them down to change the lives of generations.

As I write, the world is in turmoil as Russian forces have invaded Ukraine. Heartbreaking images of millions of people uprooted from their war-torn homes, sometimes on foot, to parts unknown is an unspeakable tragedy and cause for untold unrest in one's life. The humanitarian aid organizations of Convoy of Hope, Samaritan's Purse, and the International Fellowship of Christian and Jews serve as beacons of Christ's peace. They are all Christian organizations.

If you are a refugee reading this, I pray for Christ's peace that passes all understanding to touch your life.

Do not be anxious about anything, but in every situation, by prayer and petition, with thanksgiving, present your requests to God. And the peace of God, which transcends all understanding, will guard your hearts and your minds in Christ Jesus.
(Philippians 4:6-7)

One of Hayley DiMarco's best quotes is, "Peace in this life comes from your acceptance of suffering, not your exemption from it." [19]

How we deal with the "Whys" and "Who" we look to for peace defines our character.

However, when such things as unprovoked war removes you from your home, it seems impossible to understand. Why? Perhaps a wildfire has taken your home, perhaps you or your fiancé/husband have been involved in an accident that was not your fault, or a pandemic was unleashed by a foreign country. When such trials come, we ask God, "Why?" *The whys of this world can be overwhelming if we let them. How we deal with the "Whys" and "Who" we look to for peace defines our character.*

I caused the disaster of a first marriage and only have myself to blame. I was neither prayerful nor calm.

As most women prepare for their wedding, they ask their closest friends to be their maid/matron of honor and bridesmaids. When I began planning my first wedding, I forgot one simple fact. I really didn't have any friends! My sister was my matron of honor, but she had no choice. I only needed two more bridesmaids as my fiancé had three friends he wanted as ushers. I asked two women I knew in high school and begrudgingly they accepted. I could tell that they hated every minute of it. Honestly, I don't even think I thanked them. I got ensnared in the wedding showers, the presents, the venue, the caterer, the cake, and of course the dress. Don't get me wrong, the tea-length pink bridesmaid dresses were adorable. Thinking about it now, there was no doubt I was a "bridezilla" before the term became a buzzword.

The wild stories we hear of bridezillas mean these women are neither prayerful nor calm. During my many searches to prepare to write this guide, a couple of bridezilla stories popped up online and I couldn't resist sharing them.

"A bride and groom came into the store to get tuxedos. She said, 'I need a penguin suit for my fiancé.' Now I didn't give this too much thought, as that's not a particularly uncommon phrase. But then she pulled out a picture of a penguin and I had to match that. She made him get a tails jacket and black vest, spent over an hour figuring out what shoes looked the most like flippers, and then made me special order a shade of orange bow tie that most closely matched the penguin's little scruff thing. The seven shades of orange we had were not acceptable. She mentioned to me in our conversation that she made her boyfriend make a 300-dollar donation to the local zoo so that he could propose to her in the penguin tank. Lady was crazy." [20]

"I worked as a bridal fitting assistant in a wedding dress shop and honestly, 99% of the customers we had were absolutely lovely. People were so happy, especially if they'd just got engaged and were looking at dresses for the first time, that we rarely had bridezillas. Probably the worst I ever saw was a woman who claimed her fiancé had died so she wanted a refund…then she came back in demanding the same dress back because they'd made up. Turns out he wasn't dead after all." [21]

Yikes! Truly there is so much nonsense with weddings, it's a wonder couples can survive much past the wedding itself. Speaking of surviving, one of my dearest sisters in Christ shared with me a honeymoon story that I felt was fitting here. As well as I know my Christian sister, I'm confident she and her husband prayed their way through their experience and maintained a sense of calm. If you have interesting or fun stories of how you and your new husband survived your wedding/honeymoon, we'd love to hear. Go to our website – GodsGraceandGrit.com and post in our blog.

Although Mike and Debbie weren't traveling in an RV, I can't help but think of that funny movie with Robin Williams when I read their story!

After spending several honeymoon days in the Gatlinburg area of the Smoky Mountains, it was time to head back home. The plan was to take the Blue Ridge Mountain Parkway and enjoy this scenic route. It was midafternoon, we were low on fuel, and the line at the gas station was very long. So, not a problem, we would just get fuel up on the Parkway. So off we headed into the mountains. It became apparent once we were on the Parkway that towns and, more importantly, gas stations simply did not exist as hoped. As darkness was upon us now, we turned our car engine off as we sped down hill and only started it again to go up the next hill. To say the least, this was an exhilarating experience, and we were the only ones left on the road at this time of night to enjoy it.

Finally, we coasted into a gas station, motel (inn) combination. However, no one came out to pump gas into our car. (These were the days that gas station attendants pumped the gas for you.) So, we went into the inn lobby to inquire about filling the tank for our car, only to be told the gas station had just closed and would not be open again until tomorrow. But if we could coast the next fifteen miles, there was a gas station that would be open for us. Well, we told the innkeeper, he did not understand, coasting for miles is how we got here, and we did not want to risk any more fuel-less driving tonight in the dark.

We said, "We will just stay here at the inn for the night instead." Problem solved, or so we thought until he told us no rooms were available. We were then again told to coast the next fifteen miles for gas. Well, that did not sit well with us, so we simply told him we would just sleep in their lobby for the night. It was a stand-off!

After a while, the innkeeper went into a back office. When he came out, a key was in his hand. If we did not mind, he would put us up in a cabin with only a fireplace for heat. It was already chilly and expected to get colder. We looked at each other for a second, then said, we will take it! So, off we headed to the cabin with each of us carrying firewood. He told us to walk directly behind him as we trekked up the hill to our cabin.

Once inside, he helped get a fire going to keep us comfortable for the night. We stayed warm in this very nicely appointed cabin and woke up early the next morning to get breakfast and gas. When we stepped outside to take in the mountains, we realized why he told us to follow him directly and to not try and walk beside him on our previous night's journey to the cabin.

It turns out, the trail we were on was very narrow and one step to the left would have landed us into a deep ravine. We were thankful for his good instructions and that we had paid attention too.

This adventure was undoubtedly one of the highlights on our honeymoon and to this day, we reflect on what a great and romantic night this cabin stay became in our lives. And, now we continue our adventures together as we celebrate fifty years of marriage. It truly has been a blessing from God that we were brought together. Amen!

In times of upheaval, chaos, and strife, it is such a comfort having the Prince of Peace to calm our hearts. It's also of great comfort to have your husband for strength, but they need us even more. Remember we are to be their helpmates.

The LORD God said, "It is not good for the man to be alone.
I will make a helper suitable for him."
(Genesis 2:18)

We were designed by our Creator to be of good help. Let's not forget that on our survival journey.

Remember John and Abigail Adams? In considering their relationship, it was clear she was truly the best of helpmates. She couldn't attend his presidential inauguration ceremony as she was taking care of his mother, but just before the ceremony he wrote to her, "I never wanted you more in my life. The times are critical and dangerous, and I must have you here to assist me…You must leave our farm to the mercy of the winds … I can do nothing without you." [22]

We must always remember how important it is to find the grit, the rigor or strength from God to live our lives not just for our own benefit but for the benefit of the man to whom we said, "I will/I do."

A Suitable Helper

Carolyn always sets it up so easy for me to come in and share my heart with you. Do you feel like you are a suitable helper for your fiancé/spouse? This may seem like an odd question, but I want you to really think about it. When you go through your vows, I want you to think about the words. You may write your own (like my husband and I did) or you may go with traditional vows. Either way, those words are important. It is a commitment you are making to God and to your spouse. When Joseph and I decided to elope, we also chose to hand-write our own vows for our small, forested ceremony. As a writer, I thought for sure I had the best vows, but Joseph blew me away. I wanted to share with you, his vows. His commitment today is as fresh and new as the day he wrote these. I pray you have such blessings as you step into the role of wife and "suitable helper."

> Tiarra,
>
> As we take this step, I hope you know that you and the girls are the best thing that has ever happened to me. When I met you, my life goals existed merely to provide a bigger picture for me to pursue. I didn't want any kids. I didn't want responsibility to anyone, because I had been through the experience that people only tend to hold you back.
>
> You and the girls have given meaning to my life that is both real and refreshing. Solid and grace giving. You have given me a chance to see that I am strong. But also, wise enough to know when to use it.
>
> The chance to use everything that I have learned and apply it to something meaningful. More than all of that, in you, I have found a safe haven. A place to find comfort when I am battered and bruised. A place to catch my breath when the world has me winded.
>
> I promise to keep you. To protect and cherish this bond, support you. You are my partner in everything. My lover, my friend, my soul mate. I love you so much, and I am excited beyond words for our life together.

Tiarra and Debbie are blessed by God with an enduring love and joy in their marriages but clearly, they understand the importance of peace. As this life swirls around them, they are two of my "go-to" prayer warriors and amazing helpmates to their husbands. They understand through the trials of this life that there is but One to turn to for peace. The acrostic God gave me for PEACE is: **Prayerfully Exude A Calm Existence.**

On a scale of one to ten, with ten being the calmest, how would you rate yourself in the peace category?

Are you running around like a chicken with its head cut off? Are you making God and your husband your priority? List three reasons why you can't find Christ's peace.

1._____

2. _____

3. _____

Now what? You tell me. I can't imagine any reason that should keep you from God's peace. Perhaps you will consider reevaluating your priorities. None of us are promised tomorrow.

- Pause and pray.

- Pray for discernment to focus your heart on all things God.

- Pray for the Holy Spirit to guide you daily regardless of your circumstances.

- Don't react, instead be still.

Did you know the phrase "Be still" is referenced 124 times in the New International Version of the Bible? [23]

There's a reason God calls us to stillness. It allows us that opportunity to draw closer to Him. *But, Carolyn, I don't have time to be still.* Really? You don't have time for your Creator? *Don't expect to find His peace if you don't find time for Him.* Do you spend time worshipping Him? Do you read His Word? Do you pray either by yourself or with your fiancé/husband? Tell me what else can be more important? We pray you find peace in your struggle. We pray you draw closer to God. We pray you find your purpose for Him so that you will realize that all the Prince of Peace wants is you.

Now may the Lord of peace himself give you peace at all
times and in every way. The Lord be with all of you.
(2 Thessalonians 3:16)

Mirror Mirror on the Wall ...

Do I make time
for Jesus and
allow Him to
give me peace?

I have told you these things, so that in me you may have peace.
In this world you will have trouble. But take heart!
I have overcome the world.

~JOHN 16:33

Survival Tip #6

God's purpose for our lives is far greater than we can comprehend.

In him we have redemption through his blood,
the forgiveness of sins, in accordance with the riches
of God's grace that he lavished on us...
~EPHESIANS 1:7-8

An article from Brides.com indicates that the honeymoon phase is "an early part of a couple's relationship where everything seems care-free and happy. It usually lasts from six months to two years and can be marked with lots of laughs, intimacy, and fun dates." [24]

Wow, did Bob and I have fun during this phase—fancy restaurants, professional baseball games, getaway weekends, concerts, and shopping sprees just because. I've never enjoyed cooking and have never been good at it, but Bob never seemed to mind. I'd never known such happiness.

After we got engaged, Bob remodeled his existing condominium where he and his first wife lived, knowing we would live there too. His first wife passed away from bone cancer.

We had so much fun picking paint color, furniture, carpet, and decorations. Bob has a great eye for color palettes and décor. Truly there's nothing he couldn't do.

The therapist who wrote the Brides.com article also says, "Perhaps the biggest reason the honeymoon phase is so exciting is that it's too soon to know the partner's full personality, with all its positives and negatives ... everyone has faults." [25] This therapist never met my Bob. If you looked up the word *gentleman* in Wikipedia, you'd see two words, *Bob Snelling*. Well, probably not, but this man always carried an extra handkerchief in his pocket in the event I happened to get something in my eye, teared up, or had an unexpected runny nose. It was part of his nature to always think of me! In my eyes he has no faults!

It always seems that when we are looking at ourselves, we can see our flaws so clearly. When I looked at Bob, I saw my perfect mate. When I looked at myself, I felt overwhelmed by my many flaws. I felt unlovable, lacking true joy, chaotic, impatient, unkind, lacking real goodness, faithless, critical, and bereft of self-control ... notice a pattern? None of the Fruit of the Spirit. Like many people, when we became a couple Bob's parents were concerned for our age difference. His mother was very protective. I think women who have taken advantage of older men have given those of us who just found our match a bad name. I don't negate her natural reaction.

Like all the women in my life, the relationship with her was no different. I was a spoiled brat. If only every mother-in-law and daughter-in-law could enjoy the relationship that Naomi and Ruth shared. In Hebrew, Naomi means "pleasant one." Ruth means, "friendship." It shouldn't be a surprise to any student of the Bible that Jesus would descend from such a woman as Ruth who truly was an amazing friend.

Among the most beautiful words in the Bible come from Ruth to Naomi:

But Ruth replied, "Don't urge me to leave you or to turn back from you. Where you go, I will go, and where you stay, I will stay. Your people will be my people and your God my God." (Ruth 1:16)

Ruth was a Moabite woman. Moabites were enemies of the Israelites. Yet Naomi's sons both married Moabite women and Naomi stayed with them. When Naomi's husband and two sons died, she encouraged both of her daughters-in-law to go back to their own people. The scene was one that was intense, to say the least. After an emotional embrace, one daughter-in-law went back to her home. Not Ruth. Ruth was determined to stay and return to Naomi's homeland with her.

Any time we hear stories like this from God's Word, it's important to consider a simple fact. God's purpose for our lives is far greater than we can comprehend.

God's purpose for our lives is far greater than we can comprehend.

On the surface, we would imagine that by showing the love Ruth had for Naomi, it would serve as a fitting example for new daughters-in-law and new mothers-in-law. Upon closer inspection the story reveals how God used Naomi to encourage Ruth in approaching the man who would be her new husband, Boaz. How many mothers-in-law would want to "fix up" their former daughters-in-law? Through this "hook up," Ruth's great-grandson is none other than King David—a man after God's own heart. Of course, that lineage leads to King Jesus.

Finally, we see God introducing us to the idea that His love is not just for the Israelite. It is for the Gentile too! It is for everyone who chooses to say yes to Jesus, yes to His perfect love. The great nineteenth-century Baptist preacher Charles Spurgeon says this of God's love:

"Love is a very practical virtue, and yet it is so rich and rare that God alone is its author. None but a heavenly power can produce it; the love of the world is sorry stuff." [26]

Interestingly, when Naomi initially returned home with Ruth, they were greeted by her family and they called her by name, and she insisted:

"Don't call me Naomi," she told them. "Call me Mara because the Almighty has made my life very bitter. I went away full, but the Lord has brought me back empty. Why call me Naomi? The Lord has afflicted me; the Almighty has brought misfortune upon me." (Ruth 1:20-21)

She was understandably upset, having lost both her husband and two sons. How many of us during loss and grief have been upset with the Lord? Imagine the joy after Ruth and Boaz ultimately married, as Naomi had the privilege of holding her grandson, Obed, in her arms!

Obed, the father of Jesse, Jesse the father of David. She obviously did not know the lineage that would spawn the Savior of the world, but she knew love and joy. I dare say, able to let go of her bitterness, she knew peace as well.

The women said to Naomi, "Praise be to the Lord, who this day has not left you without a guardian-redeemer. May he become famous throughout Israel! He will renew your life and sustain you in your old age. For your daughter-in-law, who loves you and who is better to you than seven sons, has given him birth." (Ruth 4:14-15)

A fairytale life come true for her … and a lesson in the "better" for us as well.

As for Ruth's part, we certainly see in her patience with her life in general, despite losing her husband and traveling to a new land. Her goodness, kindness, faithfulness, and self-control toward Naomi are evident, along with her humble nature. It's no wonder this woman would spawn a King.

The book of Ruth is one of my favorites as it's not only rich in storyline, but it demonstrates all the Fruit of the Spirit so perfectly – for those willing to look. Ruth is a perfect example of the "better" we should strive for in our lives and our marriages.

While Naomi had bitterness in her journey, author Sara Hagerty experienced her own bitterness—perhaps known to some of you—"barrenness." Although she accepted Christ at fifteen, she says of her husband, "Nate was everything I worked so hard not to be. He was unbridled. It was as if I knew that joining myself to Nate meant I couldn't stay who I was or where I was." [27] While on their honeymoon she says, "I had just said yes to a life of husband and wife, unaware of how that covenant might work its way into my understanding not just of Nate or myself but of God." [28]

If you are single, or considering marriage (or remarriage), are you ready to release any past bitterness to understand God? Until you release the bitterness, you can't understand Him, and you won't. Bitterness will surely seep into your marriage. Hagerty's book, *Every Bitter Thing Is Sweet*, is a must read for any bride. I won't be a spoiler, but she hears confirmation from God. "Prepare. Wait. It will be a long gestation, but you will give birth. Your conception…" [29] No, I can't ruin it for her—pick up a copy of her book. You will be glad you did.

For a funny lesson in learning about the "better" in marriage, I want to turn to another dear sister in Christ, Amy. Here's her story.

Our first Valentine's Day as a married couple . . . I was twenty-one, he was twenty-two. We were both still in college. The weekend before, he planned a surprise getaway to a mountain

cabin (jacuzzi in room, flowers, dinner, etc.). But when it came time for the actual "holiday," I got nothing. Not a card, not a box of chocolates. He didn't even say the words "Happy Valentine's Day." Now, me being the very mature twenty-one-year-old wife . . . I threw a pity party. All day during my teaching internships, other college girls were getting flower deliveries from their boyfriends. Poor me. That night in our tiny studio apartment on the college campus, I told him that I was disappointed. He looked at me like I was crazy. "Seriously? I just took you on an amazing getaway." I knew it but I was caught up in the silliness of a Hallmark holiday. We had what I consider to be our "first fight" and he ended up leaving the apartment to go play a pick-up game of basketball because he was so frustrated that I could be mad about him not getting me a card. I remember sitting on the toilet in our bathroom with the door shut (the only "private space" with a door we even had!) and just crying, thinking our marriage was doomed …

> Sometimes the "better" in our lives and marriages means surviving what we perceive to be the "bitter."

Well, here we are twenty-two years later and counting . . . and I've gotten over the Hallmark holidays and I've learned to appreciate when he does something just because he is thinking of me, not because someone told him he's supposed to think about me. And he has continued to plan some great surprises (big and small) throughout our journey together.

As Naomi, Sara, and Amy understand, sometimes the "better" in our lives and marriages means surviving what we perceive to be the "bitter."

Your Story Isn't Your Own

The story of Naomi and Ruth has always hit me in my heart as something that is greatly important to each of our spiritual journeys.

During a powerful conversation with Carolyn, this story popped out, and she made it the perfect addition to this survival guide that God has encouraged us to share with you. When I think about their story, the depth of the ripples that were sent outward from the devastation of loss of husbands and sons cannot be measured. Perhaps, as you read this, you have lost someone close to you and you feel that empty space.

Maybe, like me, your first marriage left a path of carnage through your life, and you wondered what was going to happen to you. *"How is God going to fix this?"* Sometimes there can be anger and bitterness at your ex and even at God because we don't particularly care for going through trials, even if it is better when we get to the other side.

Growing up, I had known my ex-husband through family. Almost five years older than me, I was only seventeen when he started court- ing me. When you grow up in poverty, the bar truly is set so low when it comes to finding someone to be with. I saw a man with a job, an ed- ucation, a car, and his own place to live. My standards weren't exactly high. I also didn't have any way to measure how I felt about myself. Knowing what I do now, rejection was something I seemed to need in my life. The chaotic relationship that ensued filled that need. We fought on a regular basis and often to a point where he would threaten to leave. I would then beg him to stay, and we would start the cycle over again.

Abusers will often work to get you away from those who could help you get out of the relationship. This was no different. After nearly two years of dating, we packed everything up, he sold his house, and we moved our lives to the grand state of Texas. This put distance between my family and me and put me at the mercy of my boyfriend. The same year we moved to Texas, we got married. A year later I had my first daughter and shortly after she was born, my family moved here to Texas. I wasn't alone anymore.

Why do I tell you all of this? It is to set up the premise that God can work anything out for your good and the good of others. If you are sitting there with your divorce papers in hand and feelings of failure that I sat with too, understand that this moment isn't just for you! Let me tell you why.

Everything that has happened here in Texas is a carefully orchestrated symphony by the Master Conductor. When I first thought about why God brought me here my thoughts were purely selfish. Surely it was to find my Joseph! Instead, when I looked at the bigger picture and allowed God to show me how much the ripples of my decision to accompany my now ex to Texas had really done, He left me speechless.

It wasn't just for Joseph and me and not just for our girls. Had I not come here, my sister wouldn't have met her now husband and perhaps she would not have accepted Jesus either. It was through so many conversations we had here that she found her faith. They have a beautiful God-honoring marriage and the joy I feel seeing her with the man that completes her life is indescribable. My little brother met his wife here and they have two amazing children. None of which would have happened if I hadn't allowed my path to lead me through chaos before arriving in my own fairytale.

If God is removing things from our lives, then restoration is on the way!

When we are wrapped up in the hurt and betrayal life has handed us, it is easy to see only what has been taken away. We forget that if God is removing things from our lives, then restoration is on the way! Our God is one of restoration and completion. He WILL complete the good work He started in you. When He restores what is lost, you can be sure it will be bigger and better than what was there before. That is a biblical truth you can stand on.

The enemy of our lives and hearts tries to tell us that our lives are broken and they cannot be fixed. The truth is that God knows the answer to every path we might take, and He knows how to save us from ourselves. He uses every pain and every loss to create good in our lives and bring glory to His creation. It is so very easy for us to get wrapped up in our own lives and how things impact US, but when we stop, we can see those ripples and the shifting under the water and know that our lives impact the lives around us and the generations to come.

If you are willing to let Him, God will blow you away with restoration and love so that every time strife and pain come into your life you know that something amazing must come from it. We must embrace the instructions of James.

Consider it pure joy, my brothers and sisters, whenever you face trials of many kinds, because you know that the testing of your faith produces perseverance. Let perseverance finish its work so that you may be mature and complete, not lacking anything. (James 1:2-4)

From your storms and tragedies, what kind of impact do you think you can leave? Do you truly give yourself the space to believe that the saving grace and mercy of Jesus is enough? I challenge you to open your Bible and read in its entirety the book of James. Whenever life sets to seeing me sink, I know that I can allow God to breathe new life in me with His Word. The book of James is my fail-safe and I know that if you take the time to read it, you will see why. Allow the God of peace to bring light into those dark spaces you think are too far gone and watch what happens when the ripples of your restoration begin to bring hope, healing, and love to not only you, but others as well.

Mirror Mirror on the Wall ...

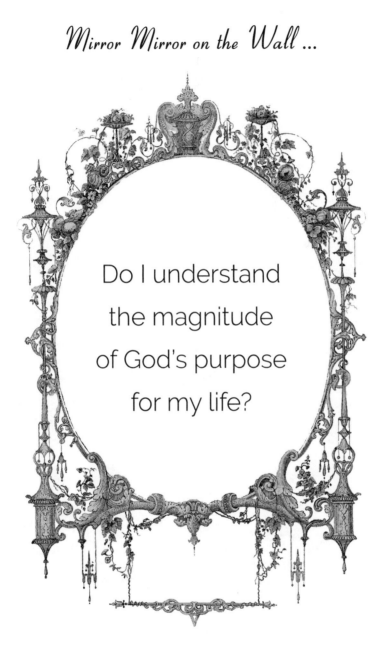

Do I understand
the magnitude
of God's purpose
for my life?

And we know that in all things God works for the good of those
who love him, who have been called according to his purpose.
~ROMANS 8:28

Survival Tip #7

When your spouse is at his worst, that's when he needs your mercy and grace the most.

If you knew the generosity of God and who I am,
you would be asking me for a drink,
and I would give you fresh, living water.
~John 4:10 (MSG)

Carolyn and I have recounted so many stories together. Stories are what carry lessons through generations. Jesus understood the importance of telling stories so much that the New Testament is inundated with parables. The very book you are reading now is a collection of stories to share lessons that can help change your life and in turn flow down to change the lives of generations. Your life and my life are just pieces of God's story being written and we get to use our experiences to make a change in the world. Even if the world we are changing is just a small one.

What is your favorite parable? If you haven't had a chance to spend time reading the parables that Jesus told, I highly recommend it. My favorite parables are the one lost sheep and the prodigal son. Grab your Bible and join me in Luke 15:4-6.

> *Suppose one of you has a hundred sheep and loses*
> *one of them. Doesn't he leave the ninety-nine in the*
> *open country and go after the lost sheep until he finds it?*
> *And when he finds it, he joyfully puts it on his shoulders and goes*
> *home. Then he calls his friends and neighbors together and says,*
> *"Rejoice with me; I have found my lost sheep."*

The one lost sheep is us. Jesus would leave all ninety-nine sheep that believed in Him to come and find us, lost and broken, and bring us back into the fold. *"Tiarra, what does that have to do with our spouse being at his worst and needing us?"* Don't worry, I am going to get you there. First, we must talk about the prodigal son. If you haven't read the prodigal son, I encourage you to flip to Luke 15:11-32. To give you the Cliff Notes version of this story, a man had two sons, and one son decided to take his inheritance and go on a journey. On that journey he squandered away everything his father had given him. Now poor and without food, he went home to plead with his father to become a servant. Instead, his father enveloped his son in an embrace and dressed him in a fine robe and sandals and had a feast. I couldn't say it better than Max Lucado, *"The difference between mercy and grace? Mercy gave the prodigal son a second chance. Grace gave him a feast."* [30]

No matter what we do, we are always accepted back into the fold.

My point to these two parables is that no matter what we do, we are always accepted back into the fold. God always brings us back when we are ready to repent and get right with Him.

You and your fiancé/spouse are going to make mistakes. You will get angry and frustrated and there will be times when you lack mercy and grace. None of us will ever be perfect. Instead, we all have the chance to come back, say we are sorry, prove we mean it with our actions, and build stronger bonds from each fracture of discord. When we don't, we leave a door wide open for the enemy to come in and take up space where our peace belongs. When we lack peace, we lack the ability to hand out mercy and grace the way Christ has ordered us to.

Get rid of all bitterness, rage, and anger, brawling
and slander, along with every form of malice.
(Ephesians 4:31)

In the face of suffering, we humans seem to place pain and loss inside of little convenient boxes. These boxes have ratings of how bad an experience is and then we like to compare those to what is happening to others. Sometimes we think our pain is worse and other times we feel guilty that our pain doesn't measure up on the scale of the suffering of others. Maybe you just lost your job but found out that a close family member has cancer. The scale tips to the person who has cancer, and it minimizes the suffering you are going through in your job loss. *"It can always be worse."* Of course, it could always be worse! Seems like that is a bit obvious. I don't care for this phrase at all. Why? To me, pain is like sin. In God's eyes all sin is equal because He is a perfect God. God doesn't measure our pain. He doesn't look at us and say that since it isn't bigger, we need less of His love, mercy, and grace. Instead, even the smallest of our pain is important to God. Read that again.

Let's bring all these things together. When you or your fiancé/ spouse are struggling, there isn't a size limit to his pain or yours. Even if it seems silly to be upset about something, you must remember that God still cares, and you should too. Men want to be tough in all situations, and with so much having changed in the world, women now feel like they must keep up. The reality is we are all soft and spongy bundles of feelings and being able to provide mercy and grace when our spouse's world feels like it is crumbling around them will not only strengthen them and their faith, but it will strengthen your faith and your marriage.

When my world is falling apart (for whatever reason), my husband steps in to provide the needed strength, mercy, and grace to get me through. In return, I do the same for him. Do I fail to do this sometimes? Absolutely! Neither you nor your spouse will get this right all the time. The good news is that you get to try again. Carolyn is going to share with you how important mercy and grace are with her story. Open your heart to see how we can truly change the world with these two simple words. Mercy and grace.

When Your Marriage Dream Falls Short

If you have an ex-husband, you may have some skeletons in your closet that you hope your new love doesn't see. Although in my case, I was free in telling Bob everything, including my wicked childhood, selfish behavior, and bitter divorce. Thankfully, he didn't judge me in any of it which is why I knew this kind of unconditional love, this mercy and grace he was showing me could only have one source: God.

It doesn't matter to me (nor to God) why your marriage ended. Once we repent, we are washed clean in the precious blood of Jesus. However, just as Tiarra has shared about her ex, my situation shares some of the same issues. During my first marriage, my ex-husband and I waged war against each other. Fights were endless and at the time neither of us understood anything about mercy or grace. We were both mired in sin.

Trauma presents in so many ways, and while I can't speak to his youth, I know that I had many issues with selfishness. Sometimes generational sin follows us into our future. It is completely biblical that curses follow many generations. Those curses, traumas, and selfishness that we can get caught up in are the enemy of mercy and grace. It may be that you are struggling with generational bondage that has nothing to do with experiences you have had. This may be your time to break those bonds and tell the enemy that his destruction stops here.

When I was younger, I could hold a grudge and be angry at the way things happened to me. That was before I realized that even the hard things, even things that hurt us and leave us wondering why, are all there to eventually be turned into our good. My first marriage was a lifetime ago. When we bring Christ into our lives, we have a chance to let those things go.

Honestly, I've chosen to no longer harbor any resentment. God has healed me from the hurts that happened so long ago. Plus, let's be honest, it's not productive to stay mad and resentment is the evil one's way of keeping a war waging within us.

I only pray now for him that he has overcome his demons.

When Mercy Reigns

Mercy and grace finally broke through my selfishness in the person of Bob's mom.

After we married, I told Bob I wanted to go to church and thank God for bringing him to me. He told me about a Presbyterian church near our condominium where they held his first wife's funeral. So, I drove by the church to find out the service times. Doing a "drive by" was the thing to do back in the day, prior to finding out a venue's information through the Maps app. There was a very small office for the pastor, a meeting room, a couple rooms for kids, the sanctuary which seats about 150 people in folding chairs, and a small kitchen. When I arrived at the church, the happiest, most humble person greeted me, Pastor Larry Vilardo. Shortly thereafter I became active in the church and on May 15, 1995, was sprinkled into the Kingdom.

The first time I heard about God's grace was from a lady at my new church, Pat Bennett. We were participants in a women's Bible study, and I was having difficulty understanding God's grace. She said "Carolyn, God's grace is 'God's Riches at Christ's Expense.'" This was the first time I saw an acrostic. I still didn't understand His mercy and grace.

In Hebrew, grace is "unmerited favor." The Greek word is *charis*, meaning favor or freely given. In Aramaic, the word is *taybutha*, which also refers to favor and goodness.[31] The first time the word favor is mentioned in the Bible is in Genesis: *"And Abel also brought an offering—fat portions from some of the firstborn of his flock. The LORD looked with favor on Abel and his offering"* (Genesis 4:4).

Regrettably, this favor led Abel's brother, Cain, to slay him. Cain offered some of the fruits of the soil as an offering, but it was Abel whom God looked on favorably. Why God preferred Abel's offering to Cain's is not immediately clear. Later, it is revealed that God accepts both animal and agricultural offerings, so it wasn't a preference in what was offered. Cain's problem was his attitude. Cain certainly became instantly angry with God when things did not go his way (Genesis 4:4-5).

While I was learning more about God and making friends at church, Bob's parents were experiencing the challenges of advancing age. When Bob's father passed away in 2000, Bob's mother came to live with us. She had macular degeneration (an eye disease) and couldn't take care of herself. I was of course excited at the prospect of helping her, getting to know her better, and doing my good Christian duty. I was looking forward to us getting manicures and pedicures together, having her teach me card games, and regaling me with stories of Bob in his younger years.

During this time, Bob and I had made the decision to move to Arizona. We had visited friends there in the late nineties and fell in love with the weather, the fact that it was not overcrowded like California, and of course the baseball. Spring training games were close to the home we were building. Bob's mother was naturally reluctant to leave her home and state to come and live with us. She was the very definition of a refugee. She was very independent and if it hadn't been for her poor eyesight, she was in otherwise good health for a woman in her late eighties.

We had a beautiful room prepared for her but I'm sure to her it just wasn't home. Compound her refugee status with the fact that she didn't care much for my cooking, and she was extremely hard of hearing. The television would blare at night. Our bed was on the other side of the room where she watched TV and the drywall was very thin, much like my patience. *Like Cain I was unhappy, as things weren't going my way.*

Moving to another state meant finding a new church home. I tried to find one and had some success with another small Presbyterian church but somehow it didn't feel like home. I loved the people, but we too were refugees meeting in the cafeteria space of a local high school. It just didn't feel like church. Or was it that I hadn't yet understood the concept of grace? At least we had the favor of God upon us to meet, albeit in less-than-ideal circumstances. *Sheesh, Carolyn.*

It is hard when you have a picture in your mind of how you want your relationship to go, and instead it follows a trajectory that brings unhappiness and discord. My excitement at having my mother-in-law with us turned into frustration and impatience with her being in our home. *God forgive me.* I tried to make what I thought were her favorite foods, but somehow, they never turned out well. I tried to talk to her about God, but my words fell woefully short. If you can believe this, I asked Bob if we could build a bigger home so she could have her own living area separate from ours. Remember, we just built the home we were in. Yet, my amazing husband agreed. I really couldn't keep my frustration from him. Oh Lord, was I a spoiled brat with the patience of a toddler.

Charles Spurgeon says, "You will be hourly tried, but the Spirit of God will give you patience to suffer long and endure much." [32] Regrettably, at that time, I wasn't interested in being patient. While living in a state of impatience, bitterness, and anger (careless emotions), I was trying to figure out just who or what was the Holy Spirit.

While our new home was being built, I remember vividly going into the bedroom of our existing home one day and picking up my Student Bible to see what comfort I could find. I came across the following:

And so I tell you, every kind of sin and slander can be forgiven, but blasphemy against the Spirit will not be forgiven. Anyone who speaks a word against the Son of Man will be forgiven, but anyone who speaks against the Holy Spirit will not be forgiven, either in this age or in the age to come. (Matthew 12:31-32 SBNIV)

In the infancy of our faith, it doesn't take much for the evil one to create upset and doubt. This scripture didn't bring me peace; instead, it caused me to wonder if I had ever spoken against the Holy Spirit in that way. If I had, I would never be forgiven! I put the Bible down and thought I was doomed to eternal damnation. So much for mercy and grace!

In the infancy of our faith, it doesn't take much for the evil one to create upset and doubt.

As we navigated our way through building a bigger home, Bob's mother decided she wanted to try living on her own in an assisted living situation prior to permanently living with us. We agreed and you could see she was thrilled. Getting back a level of self-care and independence lifted her spirits incredibly and I believe she could see my misery and discomfort. How could she not? It was practically overflowing out of me and onto everyone daily! At the end of the day, she wanted her son to be happy. I was still trapped in "It's all about me." I was the antithesis of mercy and grace. Ugh!

We found an assisted living apartment that she approved of, and we went daily to help with laundry or join her for BINGO. We even had dinner in the dining room with her. Much to my dismay she raved about the food! She was enjoying her independence and honestly, I was enjoying the peace and quiet in my home. It all changed the night she fell.

When she didn't answer the phone one morning, we knew something was wrong. Rushing over, we found her lying in bed, unable to move. We called 9-1-1 and, one ambulance ride later, we arrived at the hospital with the diagnosis of a hematoma on her brain. My husband was devastated. She came back to our home for her final days, staying in a hospice bed in our bedroom. Just seventeen days before we were given the keys to our bigger home that held space created just for her, she passed away.

"Grace is the voice that calls us to change and then enables us to yield to its transforming power."

Guilt is a cruel torture we put ourselves through when we fail. It took a long time, but I've finally let go of the pain I caused her and my poor husband. I even forgave myself, which may have been the hardest thing I worked through. While I pray that I will see her again, I can't be assured of that reunion. I read Psalm 23 over her death bed, but I don't know if she ever accepted Jesus as King. And there it was.

In death, I finally understood grace. Max Lucado says it best, "Grace is the voice that calls us to change and then enables us to yield to its transforming power." [33]

I recognized my "worst" the moment Bob's mom died. AND YET, Christ died for my worst so I could be with Him always. That's mercy and grace. Even at our worst He wants us. Honestly, now that I'm Bob's primary caregiver there are times when I am frustrated—THEN—the Holy Spirit reminds me how I acted with his mom, and it serves as a reminder of who I no longer wish to be.

Rick Warren's words are true, "It's not about me/you." It's all about MERCY AND GRACE (**G**od's **R**iches **a**t **C**hrist's **E**xpense) ... *now I understand Pat.*

It's all about
MERCY AND
GRACE.

I cannot do anything to earn His riches or grace. Jesus did that for me and you.

Before we move on too quickly to Survival Tip #8, the Holy Spirit convicted me that the work here was not finished. After each chapter Tiarra does a check with me to make certain we've said all that we feel God wants us to say. This is the first chapter where I said to her, "It's okay, not my favorite but I think we should move on." She agreed, suggesting we come back to it later. Well, it didn't take long for the Holy Spirit to convict me as to why it wasn't finished. We would be remiss if we left this chapter and didn't discuss Jesus and the Samaritan Woman at the Well.

While there is a great deal to unpack in this story it is one of the greatest tools to help us understand mercy and grace. In the cultural context of Jesus' time on earth, the Samaritans and Jews had a long-standing bitterness between them. Although Samaritan religion closely resembled Judaism, there were certain issues in which they were divided. As an example, my Student Bible tells me that the Samaritans considered Mount Gerizim, not Jerusalem, the proper place to worship God. Each culture thought the other cultish in their rules, beliefs, and followers. Oftentimes when this happens, the opportunity for discussion is limited. I am sure there are people you struggle to have conversations with because their beliefs may differ from yours. This isn't new and this inability for us to talk to others often stems from the fact we just can't get over ourselves.

Jesus however is all about others and not Himself. Breaking down barriers is His specialty! Truthfully, Jesus was not concerned with political correctness. His priority is His Truth. His goal is to reconcile humanity to His Father through "tough love." Why? Because He didn't and doesn't want one to perish.

2 Peter 3:9 says, *"The Lord is not slow in keeping his promise, as some understand slowness. Instead he is patient with you, not wanting anyone to perish, but everyone to come to repentance."*

Our acrostic, **Put All Trust In Elohim Not Careless Emotions**, is in line with the fact that Jesus knows that too often we let careless emotions drive our decision-making, such as how we "fall in love," or the nonsensical wedges that drive us apart, and the situational mercy and grace we choose particularly toward our spouses. It's easy to reflect on the situations in our lives and dwell on our subsequent remorse for how we behaved. We can't take back things that happened in the past. The key is to learn from that remorse and turn our lives away from situational opportunities where we consciously pick and choose if and how we will show mercy and grace dependent on how we feel. Mercy and grace should not be dependent on whether you are in the "mood." Our salvation isn't measured that way and how we choose to show others the same grace and mercy shouldn't be either.

If you are considering marriage or remarriage, or are currently married, I challenge you to ask yourself, can you move from situational mercy and grace to offering a steady diet of mercy and grace to your spouse? Are you going to be successful in every opportunity? Not always. But, as with all things we learn, if we choose to be intentional, we can have success. Additionally, let's constantly remind ourselves how our Savior treated the woman at the well.

Tiarra and I, as divorced women, could have been that Samaritan woman. Well, with the exception of the fact that thankfully neither of us had five husbands!

If you don't know the story of Jesus' amazing mercy and grace toward this woman, let's look at John's version. Jesus was in Samaria and was tired, so he sat at Jacob's well.

"When a Samaritan woman came to draw water, Jesus said to her, 'Will you give me a drink?'... The Samaritan woman said to him, 'You are a Jew and I am a Samaritan woman. How can you ask me for a drink?' ... Jesus answered her, 'If you knew the gift of God and who it is that asks you for a drink, you would have asked him and he would have given you living water" (John 4:7-10). The woman then proceeded to question Him about the living water and Jesus replied, "...but whoever drinks the water I give them will never thirst. Indeed, the water I give them will become in them a spring of water welling up to eternal life" (v. 14).

Keep in mind that it was inappropriate for a Jewish man to be speaking with a Samaritan woman. To add even more "impropriety" to the situation, He was alone with her as His disciples were off ... grocery shopping. Remember, if you will, Tiarra's discussion earlier about the ninety-nine sheep and how Jesus will go to great lengths to chase down the one! Me and you!! Phooey with political correctness!!

Jesus came to break through cultural barriers to help her understand how much He loved her and wanted her to have eternal life with Him. During our own battles of faith, we look for signs. For the Samaritan woman, Jesus told her the details of her life. He told her to "go, call your husband and come back" (v. 16). When she tells him she doesn't have a husband, Jesus said, "You are right when you say you have no husband. The fact is, you have had five husbands and the man you have now is not your husband. What you have just said is quite true" (vv. 17- 18).

In addition to the fact that Jesus told her things about herself which she couldn't imagine how He could know, He did it in a "tough love" way—direct, yet gentle. He showed her His mercy and grace. This is how He approaches those of us who have gone astray.

Let's pay particular attention to verse 4 in this chapter. It says, *"Now he had to go through Samaria."* Jesus knew this woman needed His mercy and grace, so he *had* to go to Samaria, for her and her latest "frog." He feels the same way about each one of us. He just HAS to come after each of us. He knows He is the Only Way to the Father.

As Jesus modeled His mercy and grace for us, can we do likewise for our spouses and for those Jesus puts on our daily path? Your response may be, "Well, Carolyn, I'm sure gonna try." At the risk of losing some of you with a line from a Star Wars movie, it seems fitting here. As Jedi Master Yoda said, "Do or do not. There is no try."

Bob has always shown mercy and grace in our marriage. If we ever disagreed (which was rare) he would be direct yet gentle. He has learned well from Christ. A few years after Bob's mom passed, God led us to an Assemblies of God megachurch that to this day we still call "home." We were immersed in baptismal waters in May of 2005, almost ten years to the day after my sprinkling. When I came up out of the water, I asked God to forgive me for my atrocities. In that moment I never wanted to be the person I was … ever … again. I wanted to live for God. I wanted to offer a steady diet of mercy and grace. Thankfully our Savior knows me "well" and is always ready for me—even or especially at my worst!

Mirror Mirror on the Wall ...

Will I show my
husband grace
and mercy?

The law was brought in so that the trespass might increase.
But where sin increased, grace increased all the more.
~ROMANS 5:20

Survival Tip #8

He gave you everything you have so that you could use it to praise Him and bless others!

*I pray that out of his glorious riches he may strengthen
you with power through his Spirit in your inner being.*
~EPHESIANS 3:16

*C*liché as it is, everything DOES happen for a reason. The time spent with Bob's mom showed me so much about who I didn't want to be. After she passed away, God continued to grow our faith. He led Bob to serve on the church's advisory board and I worked part-time in the church's bookstore and later in the HR department. I've always been an avid book reader, so the bookstore job was more fun than work. I made wonderful and devoted friends who taught me what it means to be a sister in Christ. At this time, my own mother was in her last days. I will always remember my new sisters in Christ gathering around my desk to pray for her and me.

My sister in Christ, Natalie, had huge tears falling on my desk as she prayed. I'd never known a friend to care so much that she would cry for me and my mother whom she had never met. Had it not been for God leading us to our church, I wouldn't have experienced and better understood the power of prayer. Because we were in Arizona and my mother in California, it would take us a bit to get there so I asked my sister to call the local Presbyterian minister to give my mother an opportunity to accept Jesus, which she did and then she took communion. Praise Jesus.

After my mother's death, God gave me the opportunity to serve in the church's Administrative Ministry. Volunteering for thirteen years in that area allowed me to make lasting friendships as we celebrated all of life's ups and comforted each other with the love of Jesus during the downs.

From my sisters in Christ at the bookstore to the administrative team and other church friends, I found good people who just want God to control their lives every day. Goodness for them and me is **God O**ver and **O**ver **D**aily **N**o **E**vil **S**tepsister **S**tuff. Even in the moments we think are disconnected from our marriage, God uses those moments to strengthen us as servants. Each of us can be a better servant, and through the relationships in small groups, serving in different ministries, and spending time together in church worshipping, my marriage was strengthened by learning beside Bob. How you serve others speaks volumes to how you serve your husband and even more to how you serve God.

God also allowed me to spend nine years (pre COVID) in the Kids Ministry. It's here that He provided so much fodder for writing. My heart led me to the preschoolers. Today, at sixty, I'm not sure I could play basketball and run around with them as I did in my forties and early fifties. I will be forever grateful to God for that time with His precious little ones.

Jesus said, "Let the little children come to me, and do not hinder them, for the kingdom of heaven belongs to such as these." (Matthew 19:14)

I love writing for preschoolers as they have no filter. They aren't in the least guarded. They ask questions with no hesitation. One Sunday during their sermon time we were watching a video Bible lesson and the kids were unusually quiet. One of them turned to me and said loudly in a very matter-of-fact tone, "Did you brush your teeth?" So as not to be completely embarrassed by a five-year-old, I replied, "Yes, did you?" The child then proceeded to spew rapid-fire questions. I said, "Time to watch our lesson, okay?" He said, "Okay."

From then on, I popped a spearmint candy in my mouth each time before I went in with them … just in case! Of course, when a child came running toward me on Sunday morning and hugged me, my heart melted. Oh, that we adults would just run to God and each other with such abandon.

Children are a great reminder that we adults don't need to guard our every thought and word we speak. Yes, as we mature, we don't want to be hurtful, but you can most certainly express yourself with kindness and goodness. Spurgeon says of kindness that it is "consideration for others, a readiness to help them in any way we can." [34] My friend Natalie is the epitome of kindness—**K**eeping the **I**nterests of others first **N**ow and **D**aily, **N**o **E**vil **S**tepsister **S**tuff.

The last children's book God allowed me to write is *Lolli and Pop Find Kindness*. (I was hoping to expand that series to cover all the Fruit of the Spirit, but God wanted me to wait until this book was written to do that.) *"Gee, it's hard to be kind,"* Lolli said to her parents. But why should kindness be so difficult? In the case of Lolli, she thought she might have to give something away she believed was hers. Truth is, nothing belongs to us. Not even our spouse. We may feel as though they are ours but everything, even your husband, belongs to God.

Think of it this way. He is trusting you with your husband, your marriage, finances, health, and interactions with others. God has made you a steward over these special gifts in your life. In all things, God is just waiting for us to give back to Him what He has already selflessly given to us. He wants to see if we trust Him to give it back. Let me tell you something that I think is pretty amazing. If God takes something away from you, it isn't a punishment and it isn't because you don't deserve it; it's because He is strengthening you for the future. You just have to trust Him.

Speaking of trust, during this time God taught us about tithing, giving ten percent of our finances to church. The idea started with Abram, before he became Abraham. It was the idea of bringing a tenth of what you grew or tended to into the storehouse. The storehouse is your local church. In Genesis 14:18-20 Abram, who had defeated the king of Sodom, was being blessed by Melchizedek the king of Salem, of the God Most High. In response Abram gave him a tenth of every-thing. The Old Testament scripture that hit me between the eyes in understanding tithing is Malachi 3:6-12.

> I the LORD do not change. So you, the descendants of Jacob, are not destroyed. Ever since the time of your ancestors you have turned away from my decrees and have not kept them. Return to me, and I will return to you," says the LORD Almighty.
>
> "But you ask, 'How are we to return?'
>
> "Will a mere mortal rob God? Yet you rob me. "But you ask, 'How are we robbing you?'
>
> "In tithes and offerings. You are under a curse—your whole na-tion—because you are robbing me. Bring the whole tithe into

the storehouse, that there may be food in my house. Test me in this," says the LORD *Almighty, "and see if I will not throw open the floodgates of heaven and pour out so much blessing that there will not be room enough to store it. I will prevent pests from devouring your crops, and the vines in your fields will not drop their fruit before it is ripe," says the* LORD *Almighty. "Then all the nations will call you blessed, for yours will be a delightful land," says the* LORD *Almighty.*

I don't want to rob the Lord, do you? Now, let's be honest. God doesn't need money. He needs our obedience. He needs to know His faithful servants can answer His call in the simplest of things. He hasn't asked for ninety percent, or even all the government demands. No, He's only asking for ten. And … it's all God's anyway. *He gave you everything you have so that you could use it to praise Him and bless others.*

If you are hopeful to survive your fairytale, it seems reasonable to be obedient to God, doesn't it?

We've truly felt God's abundant blessings in our lives. Once you feel this, it's impossible to do anything other than tithe. In case you ask yourself, "Do I tithe on the gross amount of what I make or the net?" My pastor's answer to this is, "Do you want a gross blessing or a net blessing?"

> God doesn't need money. He needs our obedience.

If you are feeling like you can't tithe, fear is ruling in your life. You are robbing yourself of the chance to be rich in the Lord.

I remind you of Jesus' warning in Revelation:

So, because you are lukewarm—neither hot nor cold—I am about to spit you out of my mouth. You say, "I am rich; I have acquired wealth and do not need a thing." But you do not realize that you are wretched, pitiful, poor, blind, and naked. I counsel you to buy

*from me gold refined in the fire, so you can become rich; and white
clothes to wear, so you can cover your shameful nakedness; and
salve to put on your eyes, so you can see. (Revelation 3:16-18)*

Currently God is allowing me the privilege of serving on the
church's prayer team. What a true blessing to be able to pray for God's
people. Have you ever noticed when you take the focus off yourself
and place it on others, how much brighter life feels?

It's as if the love of Jesus lights your every day. *Remember, "it's not
about you."*

Tiarra has a wonderful ministry that she is devoted to and when
she talks about it you too will feel Jesus' love and His light. I'm confident she has some amazing stories regarding this ministry and how it
has blessed her life as she graciously and selflessly blesses the lives of
others.

Working in ministry is a way of life. If we aren't serving, then the
book of James tells us that our faith is dead. I know that sounds harsh,
but let's hear it from James.

*What does it profit, my brethren, if someone says he has faith but
does not have works? Can faith save him? If a brother or sister is
naked and destitute of daily food, and one of you says to them,
"Depart in peace, be warmed and filled," but you do not give them
the things which are needed for the body, what does it profit? Thus
also faith by itself, if it does not have works, is dead.
(James 2:14-17 NKJV)*

Being filled with God's Holy Spirit means we are compelled to serve.
It is now part of our nature. When I joined up with a couple of friends
to feed the homeless, I thought it would be a one-time thing. I also

didn't think it would take very long. I was wrong on both accounts. After the three of us spent two hours putting together one hundred meals, we jumped in the car to head for South Dallas where many tent camps are pitched to hand out these hot meals we just put together. I was blown away by what I saw. One hundred meals wasn't even close to enough. There were people in line as the last meal was given out. They walked away downcast and empty handed. After about 6+ hours, I was headed home with a whole new perspective on a world most of us ignore.

I was what my kids call "O.G." That translates into Original Gangster, but in this sense, it just means I was one of the first people to begin volunteering and committing my time to the ministry work that my good friend and pastor, Earl Fitzsimmons, had started sixteen years ago during his journey to sobriety. Now, nearly three years since that first day I served on the streets with Bring The Light Ministries, I am on the board, my children volunteer, and we are regular donors. We serve over twelve hundred meals a week, and yet despite the increase in how many we can serve, we still run out of food. Why do I tell you this? The work that I have been doing is with the homeless. These are some of the most overlooked, under-served humans in America, and the vast majority of us have misunderstood biases that come from the enemy's lies.

Yes, there are drug and alcohol problems on the street, and there are mental health problems too. Yet the vast majority of homeless people suffered a life event that they could not recover from. Many of the stories I have heard began with a lost job, then a lost family, and then a loss of everything else that was left. Imagine for a moment that your spouse loses their job. They struggle to find another job and you can see depression setting in. In this moment, are you supportive? Are you praying actively not just for him to find another job, but to be at peace and find healing during this intermission in work? Have you worked to see how you can cut back in your budget or pick up more hours (if you are a working wife)? During times like this, you have to be a team.

Understand something that is very important, because your marriage depends on it. Men are big and strong on the outside and squishier than a Twinkie on the inside. You might as well consider them Humpty Dumpty. When they fall, they fall hard. Picking up the pieces may be harder for them than it would be for us. Your job is to make sure they know they are valued no matter what kind of job they have. Help them always understand they are loved and accepted no matter the hardship.

That story is one that I hear several times a week. No, I am not saying that every woman who has ever left her husband is responsible for some of the hurt and heartache I have seen in homeless men on the street. I am saying that you have so much more power as a wife than you give yourself credit for. When you band together with your husband and God is leading the way, there is nothing that you can't heal and learn through. Amid hardship, we can waiver in our faith. It is a natural human reaction. Remember that God didn't say we needed a ton of faith. Just a mustard seed can move a mountain.

Something I have learned on the street is that these people who are often invisible to everyone around them have some of the biggest faith around. They know God is with them. They pray over us just as we pray over them. You haven't truly been humbled until someone with nothing offers the very prayers they are giving up to our God.

You have so much more power as a wife than you give yourself credit for.

There is power within your marriage that God has given you to be a pillar for your spouse. Bring your marriage to the altar and give it to Jesus. Lay down any anger, unforgiveness, and resentment you may have at why you are going through a struggle and ask God how you can be of good service to your husband. You are given the biggest opportunity to serve when your husband is at his lowest.

You are not going to make it through this life without trials and loss. Marital struggles of all shapes and sizes are a part of this life too. That doesn't have to mean you are struggling with your husband. It could just mean that life is battering you or your husband and you struggle together. Yeah, that sucks, but hey, knowing that God has cleared the path and we need only go through the struggle to get to the other side brings me such hope that I don't even mind the trials anymore. I look at them as an opportunity to grow my marriage. It takes some practice and a whole lot of prayer (and I am by no means perfect at it!), but if you have Christ in your heart, you already have the whole world in your hand.

Am I a good steward of the resources God gives me?

As each has received a gift, use it to serve one another,
as good stewards of God's varied grace.
~1 PETER 4:10

Survival Tip #9

Don't let a "headache" steal the joy out of intimacy.

Marriage is not a place to "stand up for your rights."
Marriage is a decision to serve the other whether in bed or out.
~1 CORINTHIANS 7:2-6 (MSG)

Intimacy in your marriage is priceless. Now intimacy isn't just sex, though it does include it. Intimacy is about being close to your husband. When you get/got married, you became one flesh with your spouse. Being able to share thoughts, feelings, and dreams is not just important. It's imperative! Being able to share those desires of your heart (and yes, we mean the sex ones too), is something critical to the success of your marriage. Sex is just one way we can serve our spouses and it is one that can become a heated debate in your home if your sex drives don't match.

During the outline process for this book, I asked the pastors coordinating our church's Marriage Ministry what the number one issue is that the evil one uses in an attempt to tear marriages apart. Without question one of the major issues was "sex," with one partner wanting it more than the other. I asked Torrey and Tracey (our church's Connections pastors) to share with us how they counsel couples in pre- and post-marital counseling.

> The first thing we do is find out if they have the biblical understanding of sex. There are three ways sex is viewed. 1) Sex as god 2) Sex as gross 3) Sex as a gift. God wants us to view it as a gift. There are different reasons people see it as god or gross, ranging from sex addiction to sex abuse. We use scripture to show them that God sees it as a gift.

When I think of couples struggling with the gift God gave us to enjoy with our husbands, I can only offer a heartfelt note of sadness. If only I could have all those moments of intimacy back with my precious Bob to live over again and again.

My earthly prince has clearly been the primary reason I fell in love with Jesus. I didn't know unconditional love until Bob showed me the way to The Way, Jesus our Savior.

I have a love for this man that I cannot imagine another human being ever having for another. Admittedly when it comes to self-control and my feelings about Bob, I'm like putty in his hands. His unconditional love speaks more to my mind than my heart. Because of this I was always anxious to be "in union" with him. Now that such physical closeness is not possible for us, I grieve for those of you who have the opportunity for

Don't let a headache steal the joy out of intimacy!

intimacy with your spouse, but you choose instead to argue or disagree about its frequency or its necessity. *Please don't let a headache steal the joy out of intimacy!*

Sometimes our struggles with intimacy in our marriage stem from trauma. Remember that twelve-piece luggage set that Tiarra mentioned in Survival Tip #2? Many times, our experiences can overflow

It isn't easy, but freedom is worth it.

into our most personal spaces and when that happens, the effect isn't just on you, but now it is also on your spouse. What can we do about that? We can face the things that have happened to us, learn to leave them at the foot of the cross, and begin allowing ourselves the space to grow. No, it isn't easy, but freedom is worth it.

Regrettably trauma is no stranger to my friend Tiarra. Here's her story.

No one wants to speak from experience on the topic of sexual trauma. Therein lies problem number one in our culture. Sexual trauma was a generational curse in my family. You can see it spread like a disease through generations. Generational curses are an unseen killer just waiting to strike out and continue a lineage of trauma for as many generations as they can keep it going. I was no different. From creepy uncles to friends whose dads would be too handsy, I knew that sex was something I didn't want to rush into. It felt too important, too holy, and that was before I found Jesus!

When I got married the first time, I expected that the safest place in life would be in my marriage. For me, that wasn't the case. Wifely "duties" were brought up continually after we got married and after three miscarriages and three amazingly alive daughters (Praise the Lord!) my drive was nonexistent. See, just one month before I was scheduled to have my third C-section, my ex decided to have his back hardware surgically removed to see if it was adding to his pain. Now, just two years prior he had major surgery which included many screws and bone added to a destroyed L5 disc in his back. That surgery had done nothing to help his pain and instead contributed to more pain and addiction to medication. Now, before MY major surgery, he wanted to get all that hardware removed. Honestly, I was stunned.

I begged him not to have the surgery. I was going to need help taking care of three kids under seven! Much to my dismay, I was brutally rebuffed. He had his hardware removed, rendering him unable to help me with anything. To add insult to injury, he refused to let my mom or my sister stay with me in the hospital. Never had I ever felt so truly alone. The moment my youngest was born, I began learning exactly what it was like to be a single mom while I was still married. With all of this stacked on me, I felt justified in feeling "a little off" in the intimacy department.

My youngest was three months old when my ex-husband decided that he needed to detox. That maybe his medication was causing him more harm than good. Instead of a discussion about getting some help, he just left one day. Didn't tell me where he was going. Wouldn't answer text messages. By the time he texted me back, it was eight hours later, and it was to tell me not to worry. He was detoxing at a motel "somewhere" and that he would be better when he got back. He would see us in a week.

Between the decision to have surgery before our youngest was born and leaving us alone to figure things out without us, my eyes were freshly opened to how little I mattered in my marriage. What was even worse, I could see just how little his daughters mattered too. It was as if the same scales Christ had removed from my eyes had another level of veil removed from them. I could see clearly that I wasn't a wife, I was property. When he finally came home from his detox, I demanded we see a marriage counselor. We needed help. I prayed for God to heal our marriage and I prayed this Christian counselor could help us find a way. Not all therapists or counselors are created equal. Our therapist wasn't helping; in fact, every time we went to therapy, we fought in the car for another hour in the parking lot. Most sessions meant many lonely tears cried on the bathroom floor, hoping my girls couldn't hear me.

I promise I have a point to sharing this. Just stay with me a little longer.

We had a session that put me in harm's way, and I didn't even know it until it was over. The discussion of sex and frequency came up, and I explained my hormones, my small children, and my lack of interest from all of the stress that had been put on our marriage had sucked any desire for sexual intimacy right out of me. Her response was to come to a compromise. Since I didn't want to have sex at all and my ex-husband wanted to have it every day, the therapist suggested that three times a week should be a great starting point for us to get back the level of intimacy that our marriage needed. The next thought I had made me realize that I knew more than I thought about the dangerous nature of my marriage. *She just gave my husband permission to take advantage of me three times a week even if I didn't want it.*

Something that I realized after I left my marriage was that I needed to feel safe to let myself be that vulnerable. I did not feel safe in my previous marriage and that meant my comfort level in the area of intimacy was in the negative numbers. When I married Joseph, he knew all about the trauma that I had lived, and he knew it would require patience to get us through it. My husband Joseph is an amazing gift from God, and he has worked through so much trauma in the sex department, and he has done so with love, grace, and tons of mercy.

Trauma doesn't mean you can't overcome it and grow to enjoy (and I do mean ENJOY) a healthy intimate sex life with your husband. Even if you have come from a place where sex is a sensitive and even triggering subject, healing is real. I will even tell you this: while ninety-nine percent of the time I am good, there is still the rare occasion when I am distracted and when trauma creeps in and seeks to steal the joy of my intimacy with Joseph. That is when I get to claim my healing and bind the enemy in the name of Jesus. God made the very intimacy we get to enjoy in our marriage, and it is our job to make sure the enemy doesn't steal it!

Tiarra's past pain I'm sure is all too familiar to many of you, but I'm praying that her current joy is familiar to you now as well.

As Bob and I grew more united as a couple and united in our focus on our new Assemblies of God church, we learned about a Christian organization fighting the evils of sexual trauma called Streetlight USA. According to their website, "Our mission is anchored in a Christ-driven desire to shine light, show love, and encourage young girls as they walk the path of healing. Streetlight USA fulfills this mission by offering program services that combine a Christ-centered and a clinical approach to treat the whole child as she recovers from the trauma of sexual exploitation and human trafficking." [35]

Go to their website and let these facts sink in: UNICEF reports that "every two minutes a child is forced to sell her body. One hundred thousand plus US children are exploited in forced exploitation every year (National Center for Missing and Exploited Children). Thirteen is the average age a child is first exploited through child sex trafficking" (Shared Hope International). [36]

Many of these girls may struggle to know any kind of fairytale. The memories of their experiences will be something they carry with them even through healing. Your traumatic moment doesn't have to be extreme. It takes a simple moment of someone violating your trust to create a chasm in your heart about your worth, about what it means to be safe, and a confusion that something evil and unnatural like that exists.

My story of trauma comes in the form of a childhood dentist who, at one sitting, filled eight cavities in my young Double Bubble days.

At twenty-two, I was in his dental chair about to get yet another cavity filled. His wife was the receptionist seated about twelve feet away from where we were. I had a small dribble sheet covering my navy-blue suit. Yes, I can remember what I was wearing. I assumed it was going to be yet another painful procedure. It was! But instead of feeling the shot of Novocain, what I felt was his hand touching my breast as he then proceeded to ask me, "Would you like to meet me later?" Keep in mind his wife was just twelve feet away! I jumped out of the chair and bolted out of the office as fast as my high heels would carry me. The dribble sheet was stuck in my coat, and I kept brushing it off to get rid of the remnants of the experience. The last thing I heard was, "Carolyn, where are you…?" I'm sure his wife couldn't imagine what happened. Or maybe she did? Never would I have imagined this could happen. I'd known this man since I was a little kid in my Stride Rite shoes!

According to the National Sexual Violence Resource Center, "Eighty-one percent of women and forty-three percent of men reported experiencing some form of sexual harassment and/or assault in their lifetime." [37]

I went straight home and told my first husband, who went to the office, but it was closed. Probably a good thing. After that it didn't go anywhere. I never told anyone else, until Bob. Back in the eighties, I didn't know where to go or who to tell. Thank God for places today like Streetlight!

Let's pray these girls can, one day, enjoy their own fairytale… that they will author their own book as a testimony to God. Pray for God's Grace and Grit to equip them each day going forward.

Okay, so before we end our discussion on the intimate areas of life, I want to open the forest floor to a topic that gets avoided. *What topic is that, Tiarra?* I am so glad you asked. The topic is talking to our kids about sex.

Carolyn has wanted me to share this with you since we started drafting this book. Do you have kids or are considering having kids? The sex talk is something that is going to come up. In order to make sure that I was an active part of teaching my kids about sex (so they didn't learn it from their friends in school) I made sure to develop plans and rules for these such things before they ever came up. This led to the development of a very strange rule I have in my house.

This rule has saved me so much drama and conflict with my kids and one that I pray may help you in discussing things of intimacy with your children. The first bit is that most of the time when you are "ready" for the talk, they already know more than you were probably going to tell them. I tried to make sure that in an age-appropriate way, my kids were aware of the differences between boys and girls. I believe strongly one of the problems in this country is a prude problem. The second tidbit is that if you are honest and open with your kids about sex, they will be honest too. Now, let's get down to the brass tacks of this rule I have in my house.

"We don't practice marriage in my house.
It isn't because of Jesus, and it isn't because I said so..."

"Tiarra, what does that mean?" Well, it essentially means no dating. Now, before you think this is like anyone else's rule about no dating, let me explain to you why it isn't. It all comes down to the why. "Well, if it isn't because of Jesus and it isn't because you said so, why is it that you have this rule?" I am so glad you asked.

The answer is science. Your frontal lobe (the decision-making center of the brain) doesn't fully develop until your mid to late twenties. Which means, you aren't dating—or as I call it, "practicing marriage" (at least in my house)—until your brain is done cooking. I have been explaining this since my kids were little and always in age-appropriate ways.

You can judge a tree by the fruit it produces. At the time of this writing, I am two for three. My oldest is nineteen and understands my rules, still lives with me, and has thanked me many times for saving her some of the heartache she watched her middle-school friends experience. She even asked me in sixth grade why other parents let their kids date when it makes them cry so much. Her heart ached for her friends. She couldn't understand why anyone would allow something that was totally avoidable. My sixteen-year-old is navigating the waters of high school, but she too has thanked me for keeping their brains and their bodies safe from the pain of split-moment decisions that can change your life forever.

Now, the small one (my thirteen-year-old) is the kid who will try to give me a run for my money. She, however, does know the rules. Before her, I never had a consequence for what happens when you break it. My oldest two were the easiest kids. They just did what I asked and followed the rules. My youngest wants to be liked and honestly makes me question the answer to one of the parables of my youth, "If your friends jumped off a cliff, would you?" Sometimes I am not sure I want to know what she would say.

We are all human and we get to choose if we want to follow the rules.

One day, walking down the hallway, I heard her tell one of her friends on FaceTime that she had to ask out her crush the next day. You should have seen me storm her room. Like I was a drug-raiding party. Consequence in hand, she now knows, breaking the only serious rule I have means being homeschooled till she graduates high school. Now for most kids, this might not be a big deal, but for her, my little social butterfly (who is in theater and band), this was the worst thing that could ever happen.

We are all human and we get to choose if we want to follow the rules. I can't change that for any of my kids. That is their free will. All I can do is pray and educate them the best I can to the realities of relationships, friendship or romantic.

If you are engaged or married and thinking of having kids or even if you already have them, your past doesn't matter when it comes to how you choose to raise your children.

Remember the things that were the hardest and most heartbreaking about your childhood and decide how you want to approach those things with your own kids. We want our kids to grow up and get better educations, better jobs, and be more successful than we were. Let's include raising them to understand healthy intimacy and to appreciate it when the time comes for them to share any part of their lives with someone else.

Mirror Mirror on the Wall ...

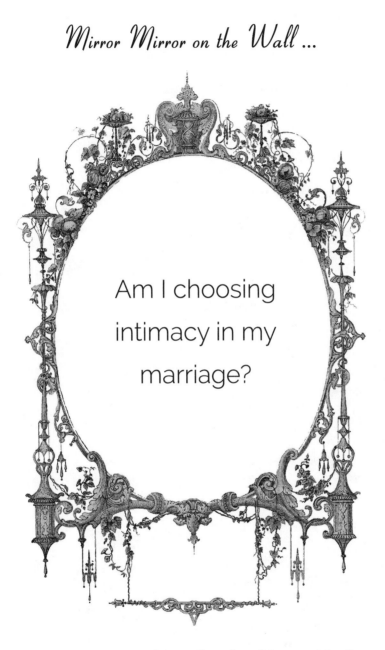

Am I choosing
intimacy in my
marriage?

Marriage is not a place to "stand up for your rights."
Marriage is a decision to serve the other whether in bed or out.
~1 CORINTHIANS 7:2-6 (MSG)

Survival Tip #10

If you are walking through a challenging time, you are never alone; you have Jesus.

Shadrach, Meschach and Abednego answered King Nebuchadnezzer, "Your threat means nothing to us. If you throw us in the fire, the God we serve can rescue us from your roaring furnace and anything else you might cook up, O king."
~DANIEL 3:16-18 (MSG)

It would seem as though getting sick is a natural occurrence in life. We all get colds or the flu growing up. Even as adults, depending on your workplace, your company may even have sick time built in, just in case. Nursing your husband back to health is one of the ways you get to serve him and of course, if you find yourself sick, the reverse is true. Despite clichés of men being babies when they are sick, I think we can all agree that being sick is the worst. But what happens when being sick turns out to be more than just a cold? How do you respond when one of you receives a life-changing diagnosis?

This very question is one that Bob and I had to ponder when we received his diagnosis. One that would change our lives forever. Years prior to his Parkinson's diagnosis, my precious Bob had several health challenges but nothing that couldn't be repaired with surgeries. However, when the DaT scan confirmed the Parkinson's diagnosis, the neurologist said, "There's no cure. I'm sorry, but we can try to help some of the nerve pain and movement issues. But I need to warn you that many of the medications carry side effects." We soon found that was an understatement. Bob's body regrettably just doesn't respond well to most medications that are designed to be helpful. Generally speaking, they have the opposite effect on him. Additionally, there are ancillary medical issues that are the result of medication and the disease. My sweet Bob, how he has suffered.

According to the National Institute on Aging, "Parkinson's disease is a brain disorder that causes unintended or uncontrollable movements, such as shaking, stiffness, and difficulty with balance and coordination. Symptoms usually begin gradually and worsen over time. As the disease progresses, people may have difficulty walking and talking. They may also have mental and behavioral changes, sleep problems, depression, memory difficulties, and fatigue. While virtually anyone could be at risk for developing Parkinson's, some research studies suggest this disease affects more men than women." [38]

If your spouse has Parkinson's or other diseases and illnesses, please go to the website – www.godsgraceandgrit.com and let us know how we can focus our prayers. Go to the tab labeled "Prayers."

Before I write another word, I need to say thank you to Bob's amazing caregivers who are invaluable to us. God has assembled an amazing team and we are beyond grateful. Whether it's for one hour or several, we caregiving spouses need time to ourselves. During the first year of his diagnosis, I refused to accept the fact that anyone other than me could take care of him. So, for 24/7 I ran myself into the ground and was truly not a very good helpmate for Bob. It took some "tough love" talk from my wonderful sister and a few of my sisters

God wants you to live healthy and with His hope.

in Christ to show me that we both needed help. If you are a caregiving spouse, God needs you to take care of yourself so you can take care of His purpose for you, your spouse. God wants you to live healthy and with His hope.

Actor Michael J. Fox, diagnosed in 1992, says of Parkinson's: "We may each have our own individual Parkinson's, but we all share one thing in common. Hope." [39] Before his diagnosis, Parkinson's had not seen the kind of publicity and support that it does now. I pray Mr. Fox has accepted Christ as his Savior, as he certainly has done much to advance Parkinson's research and seems to be a good person. However, as my pastor says, "Just because you are a good person doesn't mean you will get into heaven." God, who is only good, sent His Son so our eternal home in heaven is secure. However, we have to say yes to Him as Savior and King.

My Bob suffers in ways that break my heart and yet I marvel at the grace and grit God has given him as he maintains his wit and humor. It's because he is devoted to God and His will. Even in the crisis of his diagnosis, Bob still managed to make me laugh. On the way home from that neurologist appointment, a garbage truck pulled up next to our car at the stoplight. The company's name was remarkably similar to Parkinson's. Bob glanced over at the truck and said, "Oh great, I've got the garbage man's disease." We broke out in laughter … as that was all we could do. We didn't want to cry. We both knew there would be plenty of tears on the bumpy road ahead.

Michael J. Fox once said, "I refer to having Parkinson's as a gift. People are dubious about this, but it's a gift that keeps taking, because it's really opened me up to more compassion." [40] It's amazing how both Bob and Mr. Fox maintain their humor, compassion, and gentleness. I too always want Bob and God to see a picture of compassion and gentleness in me, a picture that is: **G**racious, **E**ffortless, **N**ice, **T**houghtful, **L**oving, **E**asy-going, **N**o Evil Stepsister Stuff.

Another celebrity, Bruce Willis, was recently diagnosed with aphasia. A *People* magazine article about the actor explained the diagnosis, saying, "According to Mayo Clinic, aphasia 'is a condition that robs you of the ability to communicate. It can affect your ability to speak, write and understand language, both verbal and written.' The group adds that the condition 'typically occurs suddenly after a stroke or a head injury. But it can also come on gradually from a slow-growing brain tumor or a disease that causes progressive, permanent damage (degenerative).' Willis' family's Instagram posts went on to say that it 'is a really challenging time' for them all, 'and we are so appreciative of your continued love, compassion and support.'" [41]

Please keep both the Fox and Willis families in prayer.

EVIL STEPSISTER WARNING: When I wrote this chapter that old evil serpent tried to take that picture of compassion and gentleness away. You would think I would have remembered what I wrote earlier about His Mercy and Grace that I thought I learned with Bob's mom! Here I was though acting like an evil stepsister. God, forgive me. And then He reminded me:

But I am afraid that just as Eve was deceived by the serpent's cunning, your minds may somehow be led astray from your sincere and pure devotion to Christ. (2 Corinthians 11:3)

When we find ourselves in a position of caring for our spouses in one of the hardest times of their lives, compassion and patience are what will keep our eyes on Jesus. It can be easy to get frustrated and angry because things haven't turned out the way you dreamed. Trust

God knows

how you feel!

me, God knows how you feel! But every time we give in to the serpent, we, just like Eve, are not only leading ourselves astray but likely our husbands too.

Let that truth seep in. *Every time we give in to the serpent, we, just like Eve, are not only leading ourselves astray but our husbands too.*

I want to do the things I'm encouraging you to do but I too am on a survival journey! #redeemedbutnotperfect.

"Now if I do what I do not want to do, it is no longer I who do it, but it is sin living in me that does it" (Romans 7:20). "It's not about me … It's not about me!" I'm convinced God wants to reverse those things used for evil and turn them into good. He wants us to understand the contrast from the evil desires of the fruit in Eden to the goodness of His Fruit of the Spirit.

The morning after I was the evil stepsister, God allowed me the opportunity to participate in our online worship. Our pastor reminded us that *"If you are walking through a challenging time, you are not alone, you have Jesus."* [42]

Here are some of the scriptures he referenced:

Isaiah 30:18, 43:19; Psalm 34; and 1 Corinthians 1:4

He then announced, after twelve years of pastoring God's church and growing our faith, he and his family resigned their positions as lead pastors. God called him to a global leadership position with Convoy of Hope. While we are thrilled how God is calling him onward for His glory, it's difficult to say goodbye to someone who has made such an impact for Jesus.

I've strayed a bit from our path in this chapter to say "thank you" to a survival guide. To survive our fairytales, having the proper survival tools and the right guides are imperative. Pastor Greg's enthusiasm and love for Jesus has changed the lives of countless people in Arizona. Just as Pastor Warren's book put me on the path, Pastor Greg has served as one of those guides working tirelessly to keep us on that narrow path and strengthening our faith. If you don't have a church home, find one. These pastors and staff members work day in and day out to make certain Jesus' flock understands who He is, the importance of helping each other, feeding each other, bringing each other to the faith, and loving each other.

Thanks to all the survival guides serving tirelessly and selflessly for the glory of God. Our struggles are their struggles day in and day out.

In addition to struggling married couples, I hear stories about divorced women and single women who are parents that break my heart. Many of these women have difficulty with housing, taking care of the children on their own, gaining the type of employment that will allow them to comfortably support their children, and on and on. It's such a heartbreak. What to do?

If you know of a woman in this predicament, take the family a meal, or surprise them with groceries or keep your eyes and ears open for job opportunities. If you are good at resumé writing, help her put one together. Is her skill set limited? Encourage her to try to get some certification or some education—it might prove helpful. Watch her kids while she is studying or at school.

I'm sure there are things you can do to help. You will know how and when. I know one thing you can do is to pray for her, wait … I know two: You can also take her and the kids to church too! *But Carolyn, this won't pay the bills!* Prayer is powerful as is bringing people to church! Try it. God is patiently waiting for you to pray more and to enlarge His Kingdom! The people she may need could be sitting nearby, or a pastor of your church may know how to help even more. The bonus is the excitement of seeing first timers or those new to the faith worshipping Jesus and praying.

When he rose from prayer and went back to the disciples,
he found them asleep, exhausted from sorrow. "Why are you
sleeping?" he asked them. "Get up and pray so that you
will not fall into temptation."
(Luke 22:45-46)

Do you realize where Jesus was when He said this to His disciples? It was the night of His betrayal in the Garden of Gethsemane. The night leading up to the time He would hang on the cross for me and you. It's interesting that Eve fell into temptation in the Garden of Eden and here Jesus is, in another garden, reminding them not to fall into temptation. And then it's even more interesting when Mary Magdalene went to Jesus' tomb she inquired after Him, thinking He was the gardener.

Do you keep your garden well-tended with the Fruit of the Holy Spirit? Or are you feeling "poor" in this regard? Just because you may not be living your fairytale doesn't mean you can't help someone else find their fairytale. *Remember, it's not about you!* Their happily ever after may not include wedded bliss.

After all, the best happily ever after is a life well lived for Jesus.

Let me now share the testimony of another sister in Christ, Brandi, and her husband Kevin, who successfully used their faithfulness (Firmly Aligned In Trusting Him For Ultimate Love No Evil Stepsister Stuff) to navigate their fairytale. Faced with impossible medical circumstances in one of their three children, they chose God's Grace and Grit.

...we also glory in our sufferings because we know
that suffering produces perseverance; perseverance,
character; and character, hope.
(Romans 5:3-4)

In 2004, I had been married to my high school sweetheart for seven years, had a two-year-old, perfect little boy and had been in my walk with the Lord for nine years. Life was GOOD. To add even more joy to our lives, I was also expecting twin daughters.

For months I dreamed of the day the girls would come into this world, for the days they would share secrets in their own special dialog, for the days they would go to school together, proms together, and giggle about boyfriends.

Then seven months into my pregnancy everything changed. During a routine checkup it was noticed that one of the girls' heart rates was far too low, and this finding sent me into emergency C-section. The next thirty minutes would change my life FOREVER. There wasn't the joyful moment of hearing my daughters each cry as they drew their first breath. Instead, I heard the nurses say things like, "Her ears are not formed normally" ... "Her palmar creases are abnormal" ... "She's foaming at the mouth; we need to scope her." They were right. The scope showed that my daughter's esophagus connected to her airway, not her stomach. And with that, Meagan was airlifted to the Children's Hospital where she underwent countless tests, three major surgeries, and received multiple diagnoses. My dreams shattered the moment that Life Flight helicopter took her away.

The two months Meagan spent in the NICU were terrifying. Every day we would visit, there would be more bad news—another physical defect, another diagnosis, another scare during the night. Those two months were also exhausting. Not only were my days and nights filled with worry and making multiple trips a day to visit my critically ill newborn, but I still had her twin sister and a two-year-old at home to take care of! My days were consumed with taking care of my kids and WORRY. That worry started to develop into anger and depression. I started to question why God would do this to a child. Why would He do this to me? I not only believed in God, but I was also attending church every Sunday AND teaching Sunday school! I didn't deserve this!

Then God answered a prayer. Meagan finally got to come home. But what I thought would be the answer to my sadness and anger only added to it. Nothing changed—it was simply different now. We were taking care of her without help—my husband and I became a tag team, seeing each other only when one was relieving the other so we could finally get rest. She still had so many doctor's appointments and tests that usually resulted in more unwelcome news. She was sent back to the hospital so many times that she was spending more time there than at home.

Had God forgotten me? I remember finally having a chance to attend church on a Sunday, and when the Worship Team began to sing "Our God Is an Awesome God," I broke down and cried. And then I left. I couldn't rightfully stand there and declare something I didn't believe in that moment. I was so hurt that God had turned my once easy and happy life upside down, and then left me to deal with it on my own.

During the first year of having the twins, we outgrew our home and somehow juggled a move into our hectic lives. We moved to a much smaller and quieter town. Meagan's scares were coming a little less often, and I was receiving in-home care which allowed my husband to go back to work. I would say that my anger and depression no longer consumed me; instead I was just numb. No joy, no hope, no friends. One day I decided to load up the kiddos and head to the park. At the park I met another young mom with three kids. We shared our stories of what brought us to the town of Surprise, and we became fast friends. I hadn't even realized how alone I had felt until I met her and shared my burdens. It was through this friendship that I realized that I had a friend in Jesus the entire time I suffered through Meagan's troubles. He hadn't forgotten me; I had forgotten HIM!

This sweet friend brought me into her Women's Bible Study where I shared my story—my happy, easy life, and blissful walk with God, and then WHAM! My life fell apart and God fell away. Every time I left these beautiful women, I felt loved and supported. They prayed for me when things got hard, they checked in on me when we had appointments, and they encouraged me to not lose hope and to not let go of my faith. To not let go of my faith. I HAD LET GO OF MY FAITH.

When it got hard, I ran from God. When I got sad, I hid from God. When I wondered, *Why me? Why Meagan?* I blamed God. I was starting to listen for Him again. I was starting to talk to Him again. One night at Bible study, we read from the book of John. I felt the Holy Spirit nudge me and say, "Sweet daughter, this one's for you." John 9 tells a story about a man born blind. When the disciples asked Jesus who had sinned, the man or his parents, Jesus responded by saying, "Neither this man nor his parents sinned ... but this happened so that the works of God might be displayed in him" (v. 3). I cried. I finally understood. My God had faith in ME, but I did not have faith in HIM. In that moment I became fully aware that I had tried to carry my burdens alone. He was willing to help carry them, to help me understand that good could still come out of this, but I had lost my faith. In that moment, I gave it all to Him. I was so tired of worrying, grieving, and being angry. So, I handed it off to Him. In return I was given hope.

The past seventeen years of Meagan's life haven't always been easy, but with God by my side, I have overcome many hurdles and obstacles, and even conquered them with joy. Hebrews 11:1 says, "Faith makes us sure of what we hope for and gives us proof of what we cannot see" (CEV). I've witnessed God's promise that His works would be displayed in her. Miracles with her vision have given us opportunities to share who Jesus is with her doctors. Finding our faith and joy through our journey with Meagan and CHARGE Syndrome allows us to speak life into families who are just starting their terrifying journey with their own child. And seeing the raw love and affection that Meagan has for Jesus is the greatest gift of all. She is a walking reflection of who Christ is. And I would've missed it all without faith.

Brandi and Kevin serve as the pastors in our children's ministry. They are dear friends and amazing examples of how faithfulness to our Father is at the core of surviving our fairytales. Brandi and Kevin learned sign language when Meagan was three and she says, "We still learn right alongside Meagan today."

If you are looking to help a family challenged by medical issues, look no further than HopeKids. "HopeKids provides ongoing events, activities and a powerful unique support community for families who have a child with cancer or some other life-threatening medical condition. We surround these remarkable children and their families with the message that hope is a powerful medicine." [43]

HopeKids also sends parents on special date nights. This mom's story was contained within an email I received in a HopeKids newsletter.

"Last night's game provided a mental break from the cycle of 'what if's' and 'if then's' that race through our brains always, but especially before every appointment. For a few hours last night, we cheered for our team, bought raffle tickets, ate pizza, and were out of our mental reality long enough to enjoy the game. When you're in fight or flight mode for so long, you forget that it's healthy to take a time out. To date each other again so you can be stronger for the future, to remember there's a lot of life outside the mental load you carry daily, to be reminded we're not alone and that there's so much good in this world. Thank you for being some of our good!"

- Stephanie, Renley's mom

Dear God, thank you for bringing me such wonderful friends and stories from women who have faith in You to learn from and love. I think when we realize how much we can learn from the people God places on our path, we know we are nearing the end of our dark journey and can finally feel freedom walking on the path with our Ultimate Prince, Yahweh.

Mirror Mirror on the Wall ...

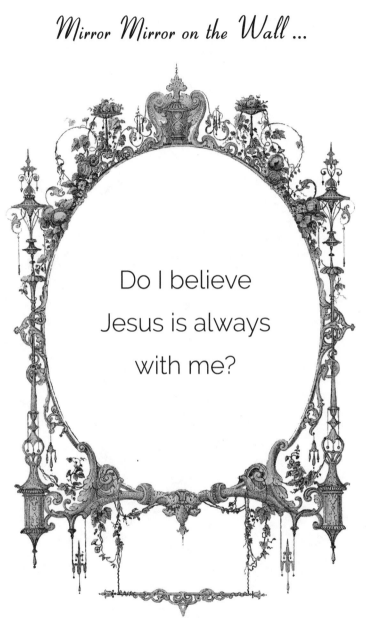

Do I believe
Jesus is always
with me?

*Shadrach, Meschach and Abednego answered King
Nebuchadnezzer, "Your threat means nothing to us. If you throw
us in the fire, the God we serve can rescue us from your roaring
furnace and anything else you might cook up, O king."*
~1 DANIEL 3:16-18 (MSG)

Survival Tip #11

Getting to the end of you begins a journey with YOU (Yahweh Our Ultimate Prince)

A new command I give you: Love one another. As I have loved you, so you must love one another. By this everyone will know that you are my disciples, if you love one another.
~John 13:34-35

It's interesting how the apostle Paul's Fruit of the Spirit list in Galatians 5 begins with love and ends with self-control. Bruce Pulver's *Above the Chatter, Our Words Matter: Powerful Words that Changed My Life Forever* is a fun read. He has given much thought to putting these positive acrostics together. Like the other authors mentioned throughout, his book is a must-read!

Mr. Pulver has designed a perfect acrostic for the final Fruit of the Spirit—Self-Control. Pay particular attention to Mr. Pulver's "L"—Let go of temptation. To do this, you must act with love and not the lust of flesh.

Sometimes we want to react
Emotion can cause commotion
Let's pause for a moment
Free from the need to lash out

Chance has a downside
Own up to the risk
Now decide what you can lose
Take your action
Remember your decision
Obey your stance
Let go of temptation[44]

In looking at the end of anything it reminds me of the importance of going back to the beginning. I had to reach an end with my mother-in-law's death before my eyes, heart, and life could understand the beginning of true love. Self-control is listed as the last Fruit of the Spirit. God doesn't do anything haphazardly, especially when it comes to His Word. He knew despite our best efforts, when we start with love at some point our actions always and regrettably bring us back to ourselves.

As David Hulme explains on the website Vision, "The Hebrew word (self-control) has its root in shutting up, retaining or restraint. A man who cannot control, discipline, or restrain himself is very vulnerable, like a city whose walls have been broken down." [45] I had no self-control either as a child or as a young adult. Admittedly I am still on my journey, but I know my Guide is the One who led me to achieving my fairytale. What does achieving my fairytale mean? Simply put it means, living a life worthy of the life Christ has purposed for me.

On a scale of 1 to 10, with 1 being the worst and 10 the best, how would you rate yourself in self-control? Now ask your mate to rate you. Don't get upset if it's lower than the score you gave yourself. Honestly, for myself I'm gonna say 1 … this way Bob can't go any lower for me except to zero which actually is probably right! I must face facts—I have a long way to go on this survival journey. In fact, if I considered all the Fruit, I would have to rate myself low. Why? Because even after all I've told you, I still mess up. I still am not the wife I should be to my amazing husband.

But now when Bob takes my hand in his and says, "I love you more than you know," I realize it's because of God's Grace and Grit that I have not only survived my fairytale, but I have thrived in the fairytale God purposed for our lives.

God desires an intimacy with us that cannot be considered through the prism of our bodies but with a LOVE that I'm not sure we can fully comprehend and that many choose to refute.

His most ardent desire is to know you love Him and that you express that love in worshipping Him alone and demonstrating your love for everyone He places on your path. Surviving your fairytale means turning to God the Father, Jesus Christ His Son, and the Holy Spirit. Getting to the end of you begins a journey with YOU (**Y**ahweh **O**ur **U**ltimate Prince.)

As we close, Tiarra reminded me of Esther's story. While the book of Esther is a beautiful depiction of God's love for His Chosen People, it is also a story of how God is NOT a God of coincidences.

In fact, Pastor Greg says she, Sarah, and Rebecca were among the most beautiful women ever. It was no coincidence that Esther's uncle Mordecai was sitting at the king's gate at the same time he would overhear the plot to kill the king. He would then tell Esther, who would tell the king. It was no coincidence that God would lay it on Mordecai's heart to encourage Esther to approach the king regarding the slaughter of the Jews at the direction of Haman. Knowing it could mean death for her to approach the king outside of a specific timeframe, it was no coincidence that God equipped Esther with His Grace that gave her Grit to approach the king.

Go, gather together all the Jews who are in Susa, and fast for me.
Do not eat or drink for three days, night or day. I and my atten-
dants will fast as you do. When this is done, I will go to the king,
even though it is against the law. And if I perish, I perish.
(Esther 4:16)

The point in sharing her story is to encourage you in your life's story. A story that is no coincidence to God. Esther had no idea when she and others went to the palace what would become of them. But God did and He equipped her.

> We can only overcome if we are confident in the Grace and Grit God gives each of us for His glory.

While we may never be in Esther's position of saving a nation, we will need to face our own personal "nations"—our lives. We can only overcome if we are confident in the Grace and Grit God gives each of us for His glory. Esther knew the importance of turning to God, despite perhaps losing her fairytale or worse still, that she might perish.

When I think back on our engagement in the forests of Big Sur, I could not have imagined the Lord's purpose for my life. He specifically crafted my story with Bob to bring me to this point. Remember, there are no coincidences—our coming together, our strong friendship, Pastor Warren's book, letting go of past circumstances, having Christian sisters to love and to have them share their stories, growing my faith and equipping Bob and me in our present challenges.

It was all meant to encourage you.

I still agree with Pastor Warren's statement, "It's not about you," but if I hadn't come to the end of me, I couldn't have written for you. God did all of it for you.

When Carolyn told me she had added the thoughts we spoke of on Esther, I couldn't wait to read them. As we reach the end of our journey together to be better and more fruitful wives, I want to share just a moment with you before I go. Esther saved a nation. Her decision to do so was inspired by something her Uncle Mordecai said to her:

For if you remain silent at this time, relief and deliverance for the Jews will arise from another place, but you and your father's family will perish. And who knows but that you have come to your royal position for such a time as this? (Esther 4:14)

You are exactly where God wants you to be right now. If you are buried in pain and suffering, remember that a seed must be planted in the dark before it can grow. Esther feared for her life. As a wife and mother, I have known many times when I must battle fear of death. Not because I don't know where I am going, but because I love my family and the life we are forging, and it brings me great joy to see us overcoming life together. Esther had just started building a life, and now she faced what could be the death of not only herself, but her people. We all have a role to play in our lives and how our lives impact others. We get to decide if we are a victim of life or if, perhaps, *we have been placed here for such a time as this.*

We get to decide if we are a victim of life or if, perhaps, *we have been placed here for such a time as this.*

As Carolyn wraps up our journey together, remember, God is a prayer away, even if sometimes that prayer is a stifled cry or a deep sigh. He hears you, He sees you, and He will restore you.

This has been quite the journey together. I want to encourage you in this phase of your life. Whether you are engaged, married, single, newly divorced, or re-entering the dating scene, God has a plan.

Thank you, Tiarra, for your wonderful words of hope throughout. I thank God for bringing us together for His glory. There are a few final thoughts I have for you, precious reader.

You may have felt disappointment from past relationships. You may be thinking, "I will never have a fairytale."

But you have a life to live.

Here are some final survival tips:

- *Your fairytale will come true by living the best life you can for Jesus.*

- *Incorporate the Fruit of the Spirit into your daily interactions.*

- *Be bold in sharing how He equips you to face all life's challenges.*

- *Remember that loving others where they are changes your life and theirs.*

You are His most beautiful creation ever!

To Him, you are His most beautiful creation ever! He has ground the sands of your life into a precious glass slipper that fits His purposes perfectly!

We will survive our fairytales as long as we have YOU! (**Y**ahweh **O**ur **U**ltimate Prince)!

In the closing scene of Disney's Cinderella movie, the new king and his bride walk out on the balcony to greet their subjects. She asks him, "Are you ready?" He replies, "For anything. As long as I have you."

As I wrote those final words, I then kissed Bob goodnight and told him I loved him.

He replied, "Thank you for all your help."

And yes, they lived happily ever after.

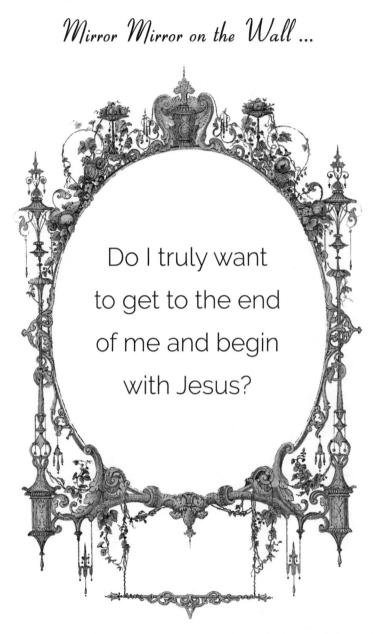

Do I truly want
to get to the end
of me and begin
with Jesus?

For you have been born again, not of perishable seed, but of
imperishable, through the living and enduring word of God.
~1 PETER 1:23

God's Grace and Grit:

Surviving Your Fairytale Acrostics

GRACE – *God's Riches At Christ's Expense*

GRIT – *God's Rigor In Truth*

LOVE – *Life Over Venom Everyday*

JOY - *Jubilant Over Yahweh*

PEACE – *Prayerfully Exude A Calm Existence*

PATIENCE - *Put All Trust In Elohim Not Careless Emotions*

GOODNESS – *God Over and Over Daily No Evil Stepsister Stuff*

KINDNESS- *Keep others' Interests first Now and Daily No Evil Stepsister Stuff*

GENTLENESS – *Gracious Effortless Nice Thoughtful Loving Easy-going No Evil Stepsister Stuff*

FAITHFULNESS – *Firmly Aligned In Trusting Him For Ultimate Love No Evil Stepsister Stuff*

SELF-CONTROL –

Sometimes we want to react
Emotion can cause commotion
Let's pause for a moment
Free from the need to lash out

Chance has a downside
Own up to the risk
Now decide what you can lose
Take your action
Remember your decision
Obey your stance
Let go of temptation.

Galatians 5:22-23

The Fruit of the Spirit Tree

Highlight or circle the pieces of fruit that you feel you need to ask the Holy Spirit to give to you.

Here's a list of the Fruit of the Spirit.

Write next to the fruit the name of the person who needs to see more of that fruit from you!!

Love	Goodness
Joy	Gentleness
Peace	Faithfulness
Patience	Self-Control
Kindness	

Abide in His Word – A Note from Carolyn

For purposes of this book's end, it's important, if not imperative, for us to have an understanding of His parting comments regarding how He loves us and in turn how we should love Him. Knowing this can also open our hearts to having a lasting love for others, most especially for our spouses.

Dissertation Excerpt:

During my doctoral studies it became painfully obvious that the lack of love for God permeates much of the book publishing world. In fact, there are those who spend their lives and their livelihoods actively and consciously refuting God's existence and subsequently the love He has for each of us. When it came time to offer a dissertation, there was only one response I could give, and its title is "The Corruption of the Bible and Its Willing Accomplices."

Some Jews and Gentiles across the globe have subordinated Yahweh's legitimacy to suit their own purposes as they have been duped by the personal disdain or false teachings of these widely read "teachers."

By using false teachers and false teaching, the evil one has deviously set forth a battle plan for souls and in many cases the battlegrounds are in the most unsuspecting places. Some will overcome to know Christ, regrettably others will continue in their defiance and will lose their souls.

To immediately shed light on present-day historians and how some serve as willing accomplices in corrupting the Bible, the words of Bill T. Arnold and Richard S. Hess spring to mind. When discussing Biblical historical credibility they choose to "either ignore the Bible or treat it as fundamentally flawed in comparison to other ancient Near Eastern sources." [46] When the words "fundamentally flawed" are used in any context to describe the Bible, the wise reader would do well to focus not on the words of man but rather on what God says about those who choose to make such idle claims and on those whom God calls "false teachers."

From Balaam who led the Israelites astray, to present-day false teachers who pass themselves off as credible authors and historians, to heretical teachings across the centuries and literary heretics, the readings from these false prophets/false teachers are incredibly sad.

Of course, the battlegrounds of politics, education, entertainment, and even Christ's Church are all tools the evil one uses to spew venom and thus detract from God's love.

Chapters 2 and 3 of Revelation are letters to the pastors of seven churches. Beginning with the Church in Ephesus Jesus lauds them for their deeds and hard work and not tolerating wicked men; they persevered and endured hardships for His Name (Rev. 2:2-3).

However, beginning in verse 4 He says, *"Yet I hold this against you: You have forsaken the love you had at first."* Who would be their first love? God, of course. As a Loving Parent, Jesus wants them to remember why and for Whom they do the things they do. Jesus gave us the single greatest command to love God with our heart, soul, and mind (Matthew 22:36-38). We can do things for others to show them we love them, but if we have no love in our heart for God, then doing things for others will eventually become a chore. It would not take long for the evil one to creep into our thoughts. I can hear the malicious thoughts now, "Why should I keep doing this, I am underappreciated." Or "I am the only one who does anything. I'm tired. Let somebody else do it." Jesus is telling us if we forsake the love we first felt for God when we repented, then all the doing becomes meaningless and will come back void. However, when we understand how much He loves us, we can then discover our purpose in life for His glory and He then promises us good (Romans 8:28). We who love Him do not do it so we will receive good, we do it because our hearts are so full of thanksgiving and gratitude for the Good News He gave us in His Son.

His Loving Reminder: First, let us love God!

To the Church in Smyrna, Jesus empathizes with their plight, suffering afflictions such as those who say they are Jews and are not but are a synagogue of Satan (Rev. 2:9). So, what does our Loving Parent tell us next, *"Do not be afraid ... I will give you life as your victor's crown."* (Rev. 2:10). An online Bible search reveals that Jesus uses this phrase, "do not be afraid," eighty-one times. [47]

His Loving Reminder: When we are unafraid, we can freely love people.

To the Church in Pergamum, he lauds them about remaining true to Him and not renouncing their faith (Rev. 2:13), but He warns, *"There are some among you who hold to the teaching of Balaam, who taught Balak to entice the Israelites to sin so that they ate food sacrificed to idols and committed sexual immorality. Likewise, you also have those who hold to the teaching of the Nicolaitans. Repent therefore! Otherwise, I will soon come to you and will fight against them with the sword of my mouth"* (Rev. 2:14-16).

As our Loving Parent, He knows we should not condone false teaching or fall into a state of forgetfulness with regards to Balaam.

His Loving Reminder: False teachers take us away from loving God and loving people.

To the Church in Thyatira, He lauds them also for doing more than they did at first (Rev 2:19), but He is direct in warning them *"...You tolerate that woman Jezebel, who calls herself a prophet. By her teaching she misleads my servants into sexual immorality and the eating of food sacrificed to idols"* (Rev 2:20).

This is His second mention in this book to the churches about eating foods sacrificed to idols and sexual immorality. Jesus knows these two things pollute our bodies. He died to make us holy in the sight of God. Yes, we are forgiven of sin when we repent but that does not mean we should keep on sinning (1 John 3:6).

His Loving Reminder: Love God and serve Him by honoring that which He alone can give.

To the Church in Sardis, He directs them to *"Wake up! Strengthen what remains and is about to die, for I have found your deeds unfinished in the sight of my God"* (Rev 3:2).

His Loving Reminder: I love you! Repent now so I may acknowledge you before My Father and you will live.

To the Church in Philadelphia, He recognizes how they have loved Him despite their little strength (Rev 3:8).

His Loving Reminder: In keeping My Command of enduring patiently I will keep you from the hour of trial (Rev 3:10).

To the Church in Laodicea, He offers

His Final Loving Reminder: A lukewarm love for Me is no love at all (Rev. 3:16).

To those who claim to be "on the fence about Jesus," Pastor Greg would say, "The fence belongs to Satan."

Remember, it is easy to love those we love, but the challenge in battling false teachers and those who have gone astray from the Lord, or those who do not care to love Him, is for us to love them. God already loves them, but we need to as well.

That means praying for them, listening to their afflictions, opening your heart to understand their desire for meaning, purpose, and a sense of belonging in this life. Be ready to share your testimony. Be ready to share God's Word.

We who call ourselves Christian should keep in mind our battle goal to love God and all His people. Within that context, we must be vigilant and unafraid when faced with false teaching. We must always carry with us God's final warning spoken in truth and love.

"Outside are the dogs, those who practice magic arts, the sexually immoral, the murderers, the idolaters and everyone who loves and practices falsehood" (Rev. 22:15). Outside where?

Outside of heaven. A place we should not wish upon even the worst of false teachers.

Lord, I pray You will encourage each reader to equip themselves with Your Word offered in love to those You place on their path. Let them share Your Truth in love. Let Your Final Invitation be accepted, in love, by those who are far from You now for Your glory.

"The Spirit and the bride say, 'Come!' And let the one who hears say, 'Come!' Let the one who is thirsty come; and let the one who wishes take the free gift of the water of life" (Rev. 22:17).

Praise be to God the Father, Jesus Christ His Son, and the Holy Spirit!

Acknowledgements

Lots of love and thanks to my sisters in Christ for
sharing their stories and insights ·
Liz Iliol
Debbie Leisure
Brandi Melton
Amy Miller
Tracy Porter
Tiarra Tompkins – Best co-author EVER!

Also, special thanks to Keith Smith and Curtis Barnhill…
Your feedback and honesty made this guide even better.

About Carolyn Snelling

Author Carolyn Snelling is a graduate of Colorado Theological Seminary with a Doctorate in Biblical Studies. She is a grateful servant at Radiant Church, Surprise, Arizona. Her greatest passion is to glorify God and to encourage others to seek His truth. Carolyn has written many books, including, *The GOLF* (God Our Loving Father) series, *Christ's Cake, The Mystery of the Christmas Stars, The Mystery of the Golden Christmas Trees, Bball, Zip and Sock: An Easter Story* and *Lolli and Pop Find Kindness*. While many of these books are out of print, *Lolli and Pop Find Kindness* is available on Amazon.

Inspired by her journey as a wife to a husband needing support and care through his journey with Parkinson's, she was divinely led to create this survival guide for women everywhere seeking to find that same happily ever after that each of us grew up hoping we could have!

Please follow her at www.godsgraceandgrit.com.

About Co-Author
Lady Tiarra Tompkins

Literary Consultant, Servant and Holy Spirit Chaser, Lady Tiarra Tompkins, has been writing and editing for most of her life. After fifteen years in the writing industry, she shifted her focus to serving faith-based authors of all genres. From fiction to inspirational, theological to children's books, her goal is the same; to help create something that will last far beyond this lifetime. A legacy that lives into infinity. How do you bring a legacy to life? Servanthood. Tiarra believes that we all have been called to serve.

As an active board member for Bring The Light Ministries, Tiarra uses words to help bring awareness to our brothers and sisters who are struggling with finances and homelessness. As a passionate writer, Tiarra shares her thoughts and studies on her website. There are many entries that can be found that speak volumes to the lessons she has learned. Through those posts, she hopes to help others see themselves through God's eyes instead of their own.

Her purpose is clear, to help others to see their gifts and encourage them to change the world with them.

Read more at www.The-Legacy-Architect.com
www.godsgraceandgrit.com

To learn more about the ministry that Tiarra serves
with or to donate to help those often overlooked,
please go to www.BringTheLight.org.

Endnotes

1. Rick Warren, *The Purpose Driven Life: What on Earth Am I Here For?* (Grand Rapids, MI: Zondervan, 2002).

2. Ibid, 17.

3. https://www.brainyquotes.com/quotes/frederich_nietzsche_109784.

4. Joseph, J. Ellis, *First Family: Abigail and John Adams* (NY: Alfred A. Knopf, 2010), 5-6.

5. Ibid., 3.

6. Ibid.,7.

7. Ibid., 6.

8. Ibid.

9. Ibid., 7.

10. Elizabeth Oakley, Professor Colorado Theological Seminary. Email correspondence.

11. "The Shekinah Glory – What is it?" Compelling Truth, accessed July 9, 2022, https://www.compellingtruth.org/shekinah-glory.html.

12."What is the Tree of Life? Bible Meaning and Significance," Christianity. com, accessed July 9, 2022, https://www.christianity.com/wiki-christian-terms/tree-of-life-bible-meaning.html.

13. "What is the meaning of the tree of life?" Got Questions: Your Questions, Biblical answers, accessed July 9, 2022, https://www.gotquestions.org/tree-of-life.html.

14. Hayley DiMarco, *The Fruitful Wife: Cultivating a Love Only God Can Produce* (Wheaton, IL: Crossway, 2012), 49.

15. Warren, 17.

16. DiMarco, 51.

17. Ibid.

18. Elise Taylor, "A Wedding in a War Zone," *Vogue*, March 7, 2022, https// www.vogue.com/article/in-ukraine-a-wedding-in-a-war-zone.

19. DiMarco, 68.

20. Maria Yagoda, "The Eighteen Craziest Bridezilla Stories… Ever," updated June 7, 2016, https://people.com/celebrity/ bridezilla-horror-stories-from-reddit-worst-brides.

21. Ibid.

22. Ellis, 178.

23. https://biblegateway.com/ quicksearch/?quicksearch=be+still&version=NIV.

24. Alyson Krueger, "What Is the Honeymoon Phase and How Long Does It Last?" *Brides*, May 12, 2022, https://www.brides.com/ search?q=honeymoon+phase.

25. Ibid.

26. Charles Spurgeon, *Spurgeon Commentary: Galatians,* ed. Elliot Ritzema. (Bellingham, WA: Lexham Press, 2014), 127.

27. Sara Hagerty, *Every Bitter Thing Is Sweet* (Grand Rapids, MI: Zondervan, 2014), 37.

28. Ibid., 40.

29. Ibid., 103.

30. Max Lucado, *Grace: More Than We Deserve, Greater Than We Imagine* (Nashville: Thomas Nelson, 2012), 155.

31. www.chaimbentorah.com

32. Spurgeon, 129.

33. Lucado, 155.

34. Spurgeon, 130.

35. "Our Mission," StreetLightUSA, accessed July 12, 2022, www.streetligh- tusa.org.

36. "Did You Know?" StreetLightUSA, accessed July 12, 2022, www.street-lightusa.org.

37. "Statistics," National Sexual Violence Resource Center, accessed July 12, 2022, https://www.nsvrc.org/statistics.

38. "Parkinson's Disease: Causes, Symptoms, and Treatments," National Institute on Aging, accessed July 12, 2022, https://www.nia.nih.gov/health/parkinsons-disease.

39. "Faces of Parkinson's," The Michael J. Fox Foundation for Parkinson's Research, accessed July 12, 2022, www.michaeljfox.org/news/we-are-faces-parkinsons-disease.

40. "21 motivational Michael J. Fox quotes on living with Parkinson's Disease," Parkinson's Life, accessed July 12, 2022, https://parkinsonslife.eu/21-motivational-michael-j-fox-quotes-on- living-with-parkinsons-disease/.

41. Jen Juneau, "Bruce Willis' Aphasia Has 'Been Hard' for Wife Emma: 'Not Easy Seeing a Spouse Decline'" *People*, April 1, 2022, https://people.com/movies/bruce-willis-aphasia-hard- for-wife-emma-heming-not-easy-seeing-spouse-decline-exclusive/.

42. Pastor Greg Marquart, Former Lead Pastor, Radiant Church: Surprise, Arizona: Sermon 4- 22.

43. "Our Mission," HopeKids: Restoring Hope, Transforming Lives, accessed July 12, 2022, www.hopekids.org.

44. Bruce Pulver, *Above the Chatter, Our Words Matter: Powerful Words That Changed My Life Forever* (Franklin, TN: Clovercroft Publishing, 2015), 56.

45. David Hulme, "A Scriptural Look at Self-Control," Vision, accessed July 13, 2022, https://www.vision.org/scriptural-look-self-control-872.

46. Bill T. Arnold and Richard S. Hess, eds. *Ancient Israel's History: An Introduction to Issues and Sources* (Grand Rapids, MI: Baker Academic, 2014), 9.

47. https://www.biblegateway.com/quicksearch/?quicksearch=do+not+be+afraid&version=NIV.

*For more information about the authors
and to order more copies please visit
www.godsgraceandgrit.com.*